CW01647215

Discover China

走遍中國

STUDENT'S BOOK TWO

学生用书2

macmillan education

外研社

Introduction

Discover China is a four-level Mandarin Chinese course, specially designed for beginners to intermediate students studying Chinese in English-speaking countries. It employs a communicative and integrated approach to learning Chinese. Emphasis is placed on communication in real contexts through pair work, group work and a variety of independent and integrated activities to help students become confident Chinese speakers.

Key features

Discover China's unique communicative course design includes a number of distinctive features:

- **Topic-driven contents in real-life contexts** get students engaged and motivated. The topics in each book are organised around the lives and travel experiences of five young students in China.
- **A truly communicative approach** lets students learn the language by using it in real-life situations, providing them with the tools they need to communicate in Chinese naturally.
- **Structured and effective learning design** based on the sequence "presentation, practice and production", with activities moving from controlled practice to personalised tasks, facilitates effective learning of the language.
- **Systematic vocabulary and grammar development** comes through topic-based practice and extension exercises. The lexical syllabus is based on levels 1–4 of the *Hanyu Shuiping Kaoshi* (HSK test) and the grammatical syllabus takes students up to the Vantage level (level B2) of the Common European Framework of Reference for Languages.
- **Student-centred grammar learning supplemented with detailed grammar reference** allows students to discover the rules for themselves through identifying patterns in the language samples. The grammar reference provides comprehensive and detailed explanations.
- **Meaningful and integrated character writing practice** groups characters with common radicals (the base components of characters in the Chinese writing system). These high-frequency characters are presented within the context of the unit theme.
- **Insights into Chinese culture**, through "Cultural corner" sections linked to the unit topics, promote a deeper cultural understanding. Fascinating full-colour photos, showing the real China, provide visual appeal and draw students into this diverse culture.
- **Simplified Chinese characters** are used to facilitate learning of the written language used by the majority of Chinese speakers.
- **Pinyin matched to the word level** instead of individual characters helps students understand how to write and space pinyin meaningfully. *Discover China* uses China's official pinyin orthography.
- **Extra pair work activities** for each unit provide additional communicative speaking practice.
- **Free online resources** including assessment tasks, unit quizzes, extra character writing sheets and more provide students with extra support.

Workbook

The Workbook provides extensive consolidation of the language skills and knowledge taught in the Student's Book.

Each Workbook unit features clear language objectives which correspond with the Student's Book unit structure and activities. A wide variety of vocabulary and grammar exercises, as well as extra reading and listening activities, provide practice of the core language presented in the Student's Book. Writing practice sections give students the option to extend their Chinese character writing skills beyond what is provided in the Student's Book. A self-assessment at the end of each unit using "I can..." descriptors enables students to reflect on their individual progress.

Characteristics of each level

Books 1 and 2 cover basic language relating to everyday topics. The focus is on listening and speaking, although there is a writing activity at the end of each Lesson 2. Character writing practice is available in both the Student's Book and the Workbook to help students learn how to write Chinese characters in the correct stroke order.

Book 1 is for beginners who have not studied any Chinese. To avoid overwhelming students with character reading at the very beginning, pinyin is placed above all Chinese characters to provide the necessary language support. However, to help students develop character recognition skills, pinyin does not appear for conversations and passages in the Workbook. Activities in the online unit quizzes, which simulate test questions from the HSK test, have no pinyin.

Book 2 follows on naturally from Book 1. Pinyin is used only in activities with new words and phrases, and the activities in the pronunciation and speaking section of each unit. Most other activities in the book do not carry pinyin. However, versions of all the main conversations and reading passages with pinyin are available for download from *Discover China*'s free resources website.

Books 3 and 4 cover language from school life and the work environment. The focus is on the development of language skills, which is conducted through various approaches including guided writing. The lessons contain activities to further enhance students' language skills in all areas across different contexts and functions. A new guided writing section teaches students how to compose natural texts by following authentic texts. The conversations and reading passages are longer, and pinyin only appears in each unit's vocabulary boxes.

Storylines

- **Book 1** presents the fundamentals of the Chinese language, based on the characters' day-to-day lives in Beijing. From simple introductions to going shopping, eating out or playing sports, students encounter a broad range of situations and learn the basic language skills they need.
- **Book 2** includes "survival Chinese" for travelling and living in China, as the characters hit the road on their winter holiday. They see the Terracotta Warriors in Xi'an, try authentic Sichuan food in Chengdu, make new friends and broaden their knowledge of Chinese to handle typical subjects such as food and drink, hotels, sightseeing and going to the doctor.
- **Book 3** takes a deeper look at China's diverse culture. Steve lands his dream job and is sent on assignment as a photojournalist to exciting places all over China. Amanda pursues her love of Chinese history and takes the Chinese history class. These experiences provide students with rich exposure to the use of Chinese language across various cultural and social contexts.
- **Book 4** prepares students for using Chinese for work-related purposes. Mark takes up an internship at a Chinese company in Shenzhen, and Yeong-min volunteers at a summer camp for international students studying in China. Both gain valuable experience by working with different people and dealing with different situations. Encouraged by his friend Wang Yu, Steve showcases his talent in a photo competition. Wang Yu herself goes to study in the US, and finds that living abroad gives her a new perspective on the experiences of her overseas friends in China.

Unit structure

Student Book 2 | Unit 3 Happy New Year! 新年好!

New words list

Target words are listed in the order they appear in the conversations.

Post-listening

Comprehension questions are used to check understanding.

Controlled activities allow students to practise the target words/expressions, and role-play the conversations.

Pre-listening

Pre-listening activities are designed to pre-teach the key words/expressions, or activate students' background knowledge about the unit topic in preparation for the conversation.

Presentation dialogue

Meaningful and authentic conversations between the resident characters set the context for the presentation of vocabulary and language.

Pronunciation

Difficult pronunciation points for English speakers are presented and practised in context to prepare students for communicative activities in the unit.

Chinese to go

Simple and immediately useful colloquial expressions or language "chunks" are provided to students.

Pre-reading

Pre-reading activities are designed to pre-teach the key words/expressions, or activate students' background knowledge about the unit topic in preparation for the reading passage.

Reading

Reading texts cover a wide range of text types relevant to students' everyday lives, such as diaries, articles, blogs and online posts.

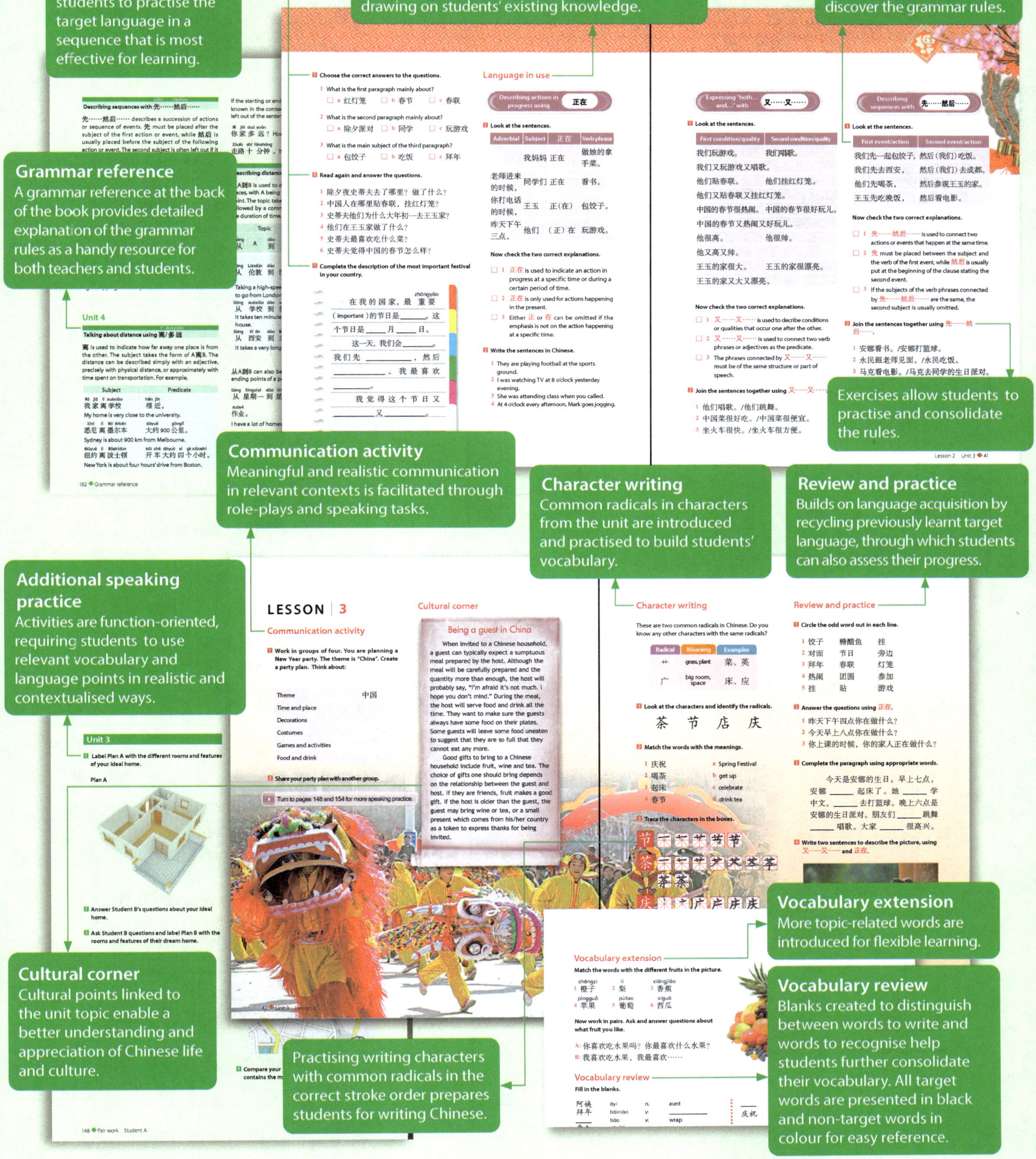

Post-reading
Controlled, guided and freer activities allow students to practise the target language in a sequence that is most effective for learning.

Language in use
Grammar points are presented and practised through an inductive or "discovery" approach, drawing on students' existing knowledge.

Short, simple examples help students analyse and discover the grammar rules.

Grammar reference
A grammar reference at the back of the book provides detailed explanation of the grammar rules as a handy resource for both teachers and students.

Exercises allow students to practise and consolidate the rules.

Communication activity
Meaningful and realistic communication in relevant contexts is facilitated through role-plays and speaking tasks.

Character writing
Common radicals in characters from the unit are introduced and practised to build students' vocabulary.

Review and practice
Builds on language acquisition by recycling previously learnt target language, through which students can also assess their progress.

Additional speaking practice
Activities are function-oriented, requiring students to use relevant vocabulary and language points in realistic and contextualised ways.

Vocabulary extension
More topic-related words are introduced for flexible learning.

Vocabulary review
Blanks created to distinguish between words to write and words to recognise help students further consolidate their vocabulary. All target words are presented in black and non-target words in colour for easy reference.

Cultural corner
Cultural points linked to the unit topic enable a better understanding and appreciation of Chinese life and culture.

Practising writing characters with common radicals in the correct stroke order prepares students for writing Chinese.

Contents

Grammar and vocabulary	Pronunciation	Cultural corner	Character practice
• The auxiliary word 得 • Topic-comment sentences • 了 as a particle and an auxiliary word • Indicating succession using 一……就…… • Words for students' daily routines	Difference between "z" and "zh"	Planning ahead	Radicals ⺗ and 心
• Describing similarity using A和B + 差不多/一样 • Making comparisons using A比/没有B + adjective • Describing future actions with 要/会 • Weather, seasons and clothes	Difference between "c" and "ch"	From freezing snow to tropical forest	Radicals 口 and 冫
• Describing actions in progress using 正在 • Expressing "both... and..." with 又……又…… • Describing sequences with 先……然后…… • Rooms in a house and Chinese New Year activities	Difference between "uo" and "e"	Being a guest in China	Radicals 艹 and 广
• Talking about distance using 离/多远 • Describing distance using 从A到B • Using 以后/……的时候 • Words for transport, distance and directions	The initials: "zh", "ch" and "sh"	The art of paper-cutting	Radicals 衤 and 纟
• Indicating possession, existence or location with 有 • Indicating adequacy with 够/不够 • Complements indicating results • Questions about sizes with (有) 多大/长/宽 • Words for hotel check-in, room facilities and everyday items	Tone sandhi: 3rd + 3rd tones	Family inns in the countryside	Radicals 方 and 八
• Indicating passive voice using 被 • Indicating a continuing action or state with 着 • 是……的 constructions • Rules and signs, history and cultural relics	Difference between "ü" and "üe"	Tang poetry	Radicals 彡 and 厂

Grammar and vocabulary	Pronunciation	Cultural corner	Character practice
• Noun phrases with 的 • Giving instructions using imperatives • 把 sentences • Flavours, food and drink, ingredients and cooking instructions	Difference between "en" and "eng"	Eating out: ordering shared dishes	Radicals 米 and 犭
• Duplication of verbs • "The more… the more…" 越……越…… • Notional passive • Souvenirs, prices, packages and travel experiences	The finals: "ian" and "üan"	Teahouses in Chengdu and *Longmen Zhen*	Radicals 走 and 刂
• Indicating the result of an action with 到 • Expressing percentages using 百分之…… • 除了……以外，还…… • Words for natural scenery, landscape features and feelings	Difference between "j" and "z"	Famous mountains in China	Radicals 寸 and 阝 (left)
• Serial verb constructions • Affirmative-negative questions • Describing immediate actions with (就) 要……了 • Appearances, features, sportswear and sizes	The neutral tone	Who is beautiful?	Radicals 目 and 子
• The auxiliary word 地 • 多 and 少 • Indicating the duration of an action • Symptoms of illness, medical advice and instructions, health and activities	Tone sandhi: 不 and 一	Traditional Chinese medicine	Radicals 疒 and 火
• Wh-questions • Difference between 有 (一) 点儿 and (一) 点儿 • The auxiliary words 的/地/得 • Characteristics, personalities and hobbies	Difference between "s" and "sh"	The Confucian personality	Radicals 忄 and 马

Classroom expressions

Classroom expressions used by teachers

2

Qǐng gēn wǒ dú
请 跟 我 读。 Please read after me.

Qǐng tīng lùyīn
请 听 录音。 Please listen to the recording.

Yuèdú duǎnwén
阅读 短文。 Read the passage.

Qǐng huídá wèntí
请 回答 问题。 Please answer the questions.

Wánchéng jùzi
完成 句子。 Complete the sentences.

Xuǎnzé zhèngquè dá' àn
选择 正确 答案。 Choose the correct answers.

Jīntiān wǒmen shàng dì-yī kè
今天 我们 上 第一课。 Today we are going to study Lesson 1.

Qǐng dǎkāi shū fān dào dì-shí yè
请 打开 书 翻 到 第十 页。 Please open your books and turn to page 10.

Wǒmen xiān xuéxí yíxià shēngcí
我们 先 学习 一下 生词。 Let's study the new words first.

Nǎ wèi tóngxué zhīdào zhège cí de yìsi
哪位 同学 知道 这个 词 的 意思？ Who knows the meaning of this word?

Nǐ kěyǐ dàshēng yìdiǎnr ma
你 可以 大声 一点儿 吗？ Could you speak a bit louder?

Xiàmiàn wǒmen zuò duìhuà liànxí
下面 我们 做 对话 练习。 Next let's do some dialogue practice.

Liǎng rén yì zǔ zuò liànxí
两 人 一 组 做 练习。 Work in pairs.

Bǎ jùzi fānyì chéng Zhōngwén Yīngwén
把 句子 翻译 成 中文 / 英文。 Translate the sentences into Chinese/English.

Zhǎochū yǔ túpiàn duìyìng de cíyǔ
找出 与 图片 对应 的 词语。 Match the words with the pictures.

Gēnjù túpiàn zàojù
根据 图片 造句。 Write a sentence to describe the picture.

Classroom expressions used by students

3

Wǒ yǒu yí gè wèntí 我有一个问题。	I have a question.
Zhège zì dú dì jǐ shēng 这个字读第几声？	What tone is this character?
Zhège zì zěnme xiě 这个字怎么写？	How do you write this character?
Zhège cí shì shénme yìsi 这个词是什么意思？	What does this word mean?
Zhè jù huà yòng Yīngyǔ Hànyǔ zěnme shuō 这句话用英语/汉语怎么说？	How do you say this sentence in English/Chinese?
Wǒ méiyǒu tīng qīngchu nín néng chóngfù yí biàn ma 我没有听清楚，您能重复一遍吗？	I didn't hear clearly. Could you repeat that?
Nín néng shuō màn yìdiǎnr ma 您能说慢一点儿吗？	Could you speak a bit more slowly?
Zhège cí kěyǐ zhèyàng yòng ma 这个词可以这样用吗？	Can I use the word this way?
Shénme shíhou jiāo zuòyè kǎoshì 什么时候交作业/考试？	When are we going to hand in the homework/have the test?
Wǒ kěyǐ qù xǐshǒujiān ma 我可以去洗手间吗？	May I go to the toilet?

Places in *Discover China*

Xi'an

西安 (Xī' ān) capital city of Shaanxi Province, ancient capital of the Tang Dynasty, starting point of the Silk Road

陕西历史博物馆 (Shǎnxī Lìshǐ Bówùguǎn) the Shaanxi History Museum

钟楼 (Zhōnglóu) Bell Tower, used to announce the hours in ancient times

大雁塔 (Dàyàn Tǎ) Big Wild Goose Pagoda, where the monk Xuan Zang kept the Buddhist scrolls he brought back from India during the Tang Dynasty

古城墙 (Gǔchéngqiáng) Xi'an's ancient city walls, the best preserved fortification from the Ming Dynasty, built on the remains of the Tang capital, Chang'an

大清真寺 (Dàqīngzhēn Sì) the Great Mosque of Xi'an

Lintong

临潼 (Líntóng) a county 30 kilometres to the east of Xi'an, where the Terracotta Warriors were discovered

兵马俑 (Bīngmǎyǒng) the Terracotta Warriors, burial goods of the Emperor Qin Shihuang, the first emperor of China

Chengdu

成都 (Chéngdū) capital city of Sichuan Province

卧龙自然保护区 (Wòlóng Zìrán Bǎohùqū) Wolong Nature Reserve, also called "Panda Country"

九寨沟 (Jiǔzhàigōu) Jiuzhaigou Valley, a place of stunning natural beauty, which gets its name from the nine Tibetan villages in the mountains

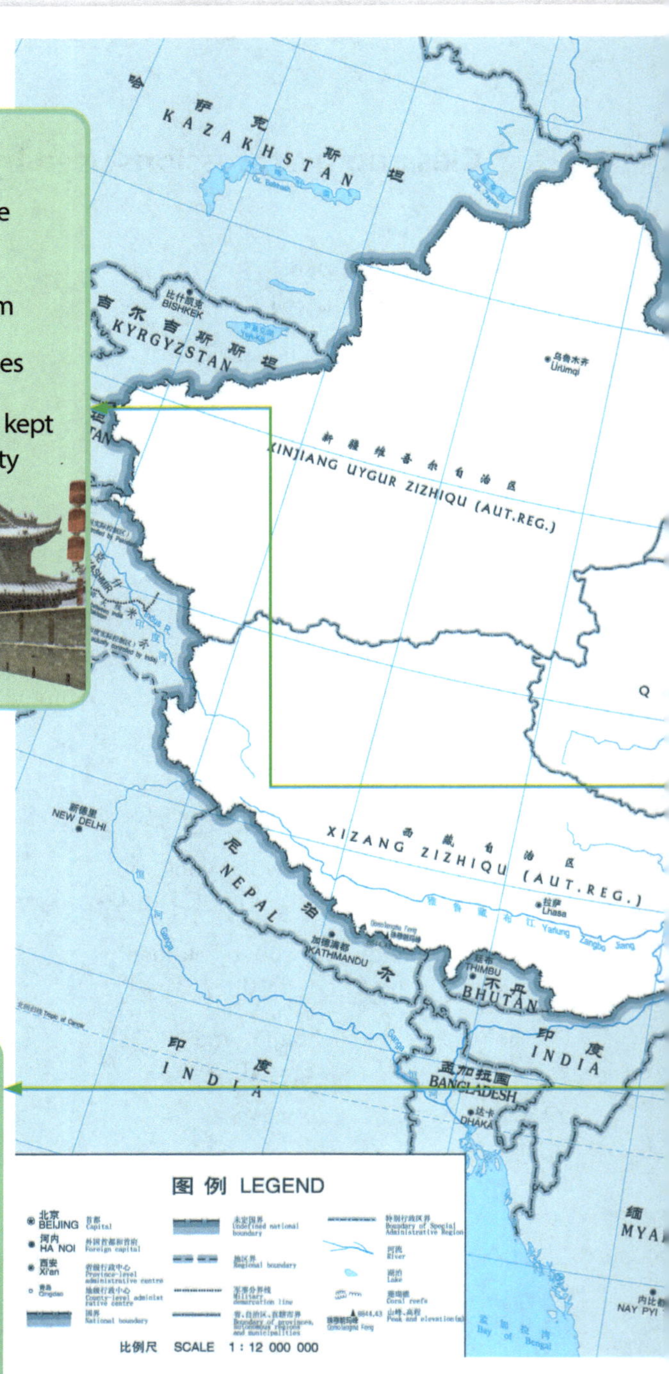

Historical timeline

兵马俑
Bīngmǎyǒng

青铜马
qīngtóngmǎ

BCE 300 — CE 1 — 500

China: 秦 Qín; 汉 Hàn; 三国 Sānguó

Europe/Middle East: Ancient Greece; Roman Empire (Western empire)

Americas: Olmec; Mayan Classic period

* This timeline does not include all dynasties and eras in China's history. The selected eras illustrate some notable contemporaneous periods in China and abroad.

Harbin

哈尔滨 (Hā' ěrbīn) capital city of Heilongjiang Province

冰雪节 (Bīngxuějié) the annual Snow & Ice Festival, featuring ice sculptures

Beijing

北京 (Běijīng) capital of China

故宫 (Gùgōng) the Forbidden City, royal residence of the Ming and Qing dynasties

长城 (Chángchéng) the Great Wall

Yunnan

云南 (Yúnnán) province in south-west China

泼水节 (Pōshuǐjié) Water-Splashing Festival, celebrated by the Dai ethnic group

唐三彩
Tángsāncǎi

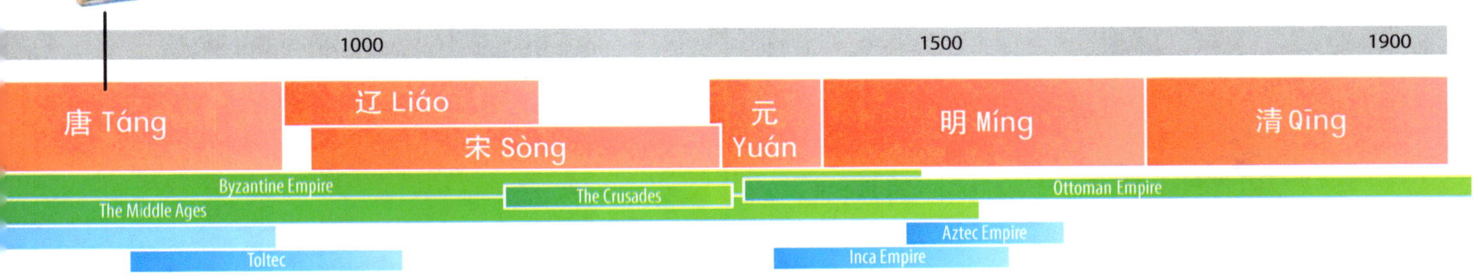

Meet the characters

Mǎkè
Mark Johnson (马克) comes from Brisbane. Mark went on holiday to China after completing high school, and decided to stay and learn Chinese at a university in Beijing. Mark enjoys the outdoors, and he likes surfing and sailing.

Āmàndá
Amanda da Silva (阿曼达) is Mark's classmate, from São Paulo. She loves travelling and has a keen interest in history. As well as studying Chinese, Amanda is taking classes in Chinese history at the university.

Shǐdìfū
Steve Brown (史蒂夫), another classmate of Mark and Amanda's, comes from London. He works part-time for a UK-based magazine and is a keen photographer. He enjoys exploring different cultures and meeting different people.

Wáng Yù
Wang Yu (王 玉) was born in Beijing. She knows the others from university, where she studies music. She has played the piano since she was five. She likes cooking and sports including swimming and tennis.

Jīn Yǒngmín
Kim Yeong-min (金 永民) is also studying Chinese at the university. He comes from Seoul. Like Wang Yu, Yeong-min is a musician, and plays guitar in a local band. He plans to study Chinese medicine after he finishes his courses in Chinese. Yeong-min likes to spend his free time reading and listening to music.

UNIT 1

Jīntiān zhēn máng
今天真忙！
What a busy day!

LESSON 1

Vocabulary and listening

4 **1 Number the events of a student's day in the correct order.**

a

shàngkè
☐ 上课

b

qǐchuáng
☐ 起床

c

shuìjiào
☐ 睡觉

d

zuò zuòyè
☐ 做 作业

e

zuò yùndòng
☐ 做 运动

f

chīfàn
☐ 吃饭

Now listen and say the words.

5 **2 Steve invites Amanda and Yeong-min to have a meal together after class. Listen to the conversation and answer the questions.**

1 阿曼达放学后要做什么？
2 中国的大学每天早上几点开始上课？
3 永民可以一起去吃饭吗？

史蒂夫：放学以后，我们一起去吃饭吧。东门附近有个上海饭馆很不错。

阿曼达：我去过那个饭馆，那里的菜很好吃！但是今天我不能去。

史蒂夫：为什么？

阿曼达：我要去打网球。

永民：真的吗？我不知道你会打网球。你跟谁打？

阿曼达：跟王玉。她打网球打得很好。你会打网球吗？

永民：不会。史蒂夫，你呢？

史蒂夫：我也不会。我觉得我应该多做运动。我住在伦敦的时候每天上课前都去跑步，但是在中国就不可能。

永民：为什么在中国不可能？

史蒂夫：因为中国大学的上课时间太早了，每天早上八点开始上课。我觉得这么早起床去教室很难。这么早去跑步当然不可能！

阿曼达：我觉得八点不那么早。我每天七点起床，吃早饭，然后去上课。

史蒂夫：永民，你和我去吃饭吗？

永民：对不起，我的中文作业还没做完，明天要交给老师。我还要复习，准备星期三的考试。

阿曼达：没关系，我们可以下次一起吃饭。

New words

fàngxué 放学	school is over
néng 能	can
wèi shénme 为什么	why
de 得	(used between a verb or an adjective and its complement to indicate result or degree)
shàngkè 上课	attend a class
qián 前	before
jiù 就	exactly, as soon as
kěnéng 可能	possible
yīnwèi 因为	because
zǎo 早	early
zhème 这么	so, such
qǐchuáng 起床	get up
chuáng 床	bed
jiàoshì 教室	classroom
nán 难	difficult
zuòyè 作业	homework
hái 还	still, yet, also
wán 完	complete
jiāo 交	hand in, submit
fùxí 复习	revise, review
zhǔnbèi 准备	prepare
kǎoshì 考试	exam, test
méi guānxi 没关系	it doesn't matter
xiàcì 下次	next time

5

3 Listen again and check the correct answers.

1 史蒂夫放学后想去做什么？

☐ a 跑步　☐ b 吃饭

2 阿曼达每天早上几点起床？

☐ a 七点　☐ b 八点

3 永民打算做什么？

☐ a 做中文作业　☐ b 复习准备考试

4 Work in pairs. Talk about your plans after class today and invite your partner to join you. Decline your partner's invitation and give reasons why you cannot join him/her.

Pronunciation and speaking

Difference between "z" and "zh"

6

1 Check the correct initials for the characters.

1	做	☐ z	☐ zh
2	早	☐ z	☐ zh
3	中	☐ z	☐ zh
4	知	☐ z	☐ zh
5	住	☐ z	☐ zh
6	作	☐ z	☐ zh

Now listen and repeat.

7

2 Check the correct pinyin for the words.

1	早上	☐ zǎoshang	☐ zhǎoshang
2	作业	☐ zuòyè	☐ zhuòyè
3	知道	☐ zīdào	☐ zhīdào
4	中国	☐ Zōngguó	☐ Zhōngguó

Now listen and repeat.

8

3 Listen and say the words.

1	shàngkè 上课	fàngxué 放学	chī zǎofàn 吃 早饭
2	qǐchuáng 起床	pǎobù 跑步	zuò yùndòng 做 运动
3	kǎoshì 考试	fùxí 复习	jiāo zuòyè 交 作业

4 Work in pairs. Ask each other what you usually do during the following times.

6:00—8:00	8:00—12:00
12:00—15:00	15:00—19:00
19:00—24:00	00:00—6:00

Now work with another pair. Tell them about your partner's daily routine.

CHINESE TO GO

9

Being late

Jǐ diǎn le 几点了?	What time is it? (Don't you know the time?)
Nǐ zěnme cái lái 你怎么才来?	Why are you so late?
Lùshang dǔchē 路上 堵车。	There was a traffic jam on the way.
Wǒ qǐchuáng wǎn le 我 起床 晚 了。	I got up late.
Wǒ de biǎo màn le 我 的 表 慢 了。	My watch is slow.

LESSON 2

Reading and writing

1 Work in pairs. Check the activities that you do every day.

- ☐ a chī zǎofàn 吃早饭
- ☐ b kàn xīnwén 看新闻
- ☐ c shàngkè 上课
- ☐ d xiě rìjì 写日记
- ☐ e pāizhào 拍照
- ☐ f dú gùshi 读故事

10

2 Read Mark's diary and answer the questions.

1 马克喜欢上中文课吗？为什么？

2 放学以后，马克去了哪里？

3 为什么马克觉得很累？

New words

máng 忙	busy	yǒuqù 有趣	interesting
chídào 迟到	be late	túshūguǎn 图书馆	library
cái 才	not until	jiè 借	borrow, lend
yǐjing 已经	already	běn 本	(used for books)
bù hǎoyìsi 不好意思	(something makes you feel) embarrassed	tiānqì 天气	weather
ràng 让	let, allow, ask	kāixīn 开心	happy
dú 读	read	yìbiān 一边	while, at the same time
gùshi 故事	story	shuōhuà 说话	speak, talk
tóngxué 同学	classmate	lèi 累	tired
yòng 用	use	rìjì 日记	diary
xīnwén 新闻	news	shàngchuáng 上床	go to bed
		shuìjiào 睡觉	sleep

一月十二日　星期三

今天真忙！我七点半起床，没吃早饭就出去了。路上人很多，我迟到了，八点五分才到教室。老师已经在上课了，我觉得很不好意思。上课的时候，老师让我们读一些中文故事。有些同学觉得读故事没有用，他们喜欢看中文新闻。但是我觉得这些故事很有趣。有时间我要去图书馆借几本中文故事书。

放学以后，我去了公园跟我的朋友李明见面。今天天气很好，我们在公园拍了一些很漂亮的照片。我觉得很开心。

晚上八点我跟王玉和永民一起吃晚饭。我们一边吃饭一边说话，大家都很高兴。晚上十一点我才回到宿舍。我觉得很累，一写完日记就上床睡觉了。

3 Read the diary again and check the true statements.

☐ 1 马克到教室的时候，老师还没有来。

☐ 2 一些同学觉得读故事没有用。

☐ 3 马克在公园拍的照片很漂亮。

☐ 4 晚上八点马克和朋友们一起吃了饭。

☐ 5 马克一回宿舍就上床睡觉了。

4 Make a list of the things you did yesterday.

	上午	下午	晚上
做什么			
和谁一起			
觉得怎么样			

Now use the list to write a diary entry. Use Mark's diary to help you.

Language in use

The auxiliary word 得

1 Look at the sentences.

Subject	Verb phrase	Verb	得	Complement
她	打网球	打	得	很好。
马克		来	得	很早。
他	（吃饭）	吃	得	很多。
小王		跑	得	不快。
你		做	得	不好。

Now check the two correct explanations.

☐ 1 得 is used between a verb and its complement to indicate the result or degree of an action.

☐ 2 There can be two verbs in a sentence, with the second verb being the same as the verb in the first verb phrase.

☐ 3 得 can be put between a subject and a verb to indicate the result or degree of an action.

2 Write three sentences about yourself, using 得 to indicate the result or degree.

Topic-comment sentences

1 Look at the sentences.

Topic	Comment
这么早起床去教室	很难。
这么早去跑步	当然不可能。
我的中文作业	明天要交给老师。
电影院离这里	远不远？

Now check the two correct explanations.

- [ ] 1 Topic-comment sentences are used to provide comments or more information about certain things.
- [ ] 2 The topic must always be put at the beginning, and consist of a verb phrase or a noun phrase.
- [ ] 3 A verb is always necessary in the comment in a topic-comment sentence.

2 Write the sentences in Chinese.

1 It takes ten minutes to get there by taxi.
2 The supermarket is very close to the school.
3 It's not possible to go to bed before 10 pm.

了 as a particle and an auxiliary word

1 Look at the sentences.

Subject	Predicate
王玉	买了那条裙子。
他	吃了午饭。
我	迟到了。
老师	已经在上课了。

Now check the two correct explanations.

- [ ] 1 了 can be used after a verb as an auxiliary word to indicate that an action has taken place.
- [ ] 2 了 can also be used at the end of a statement as a particle to indicate a change of situation or state.
- [ ] 3 The meaning of a sentence will not be affected no matter where 了 is placed.

2 Put 了 in the correct places in the sentences.

1 上个星期我爸爸去北京。
2 他在伦敦住三年。
3 下个月我就十八岁。

Indicating succession using 一……就……

1 Look at the sentences.

Subject 1	一	Verb phrase 1	Subject 2	就	Verb phrase 2
我	一	写完日记		就	上床睡觉了。
我	一	吃完饭		就	出来了。
他	一	回来，	我	就	出去。
老师	一	来，	我们	就	开始上课。

Now check the two correct explanations.

- [ ] 1 一……就…… is used to connect two events or actions that happen one after the other.
- [ ] 2 一……就…… is used to connect two events or actions that happen at the same time.
- [ ] 3 The subjects of the verb phrases connected by 一……就…… can be different.

2 Join the sentences together using 一……就…….

1 他回家。/他做作业。
2 永民到电影院。/电影开始了。
3 她开始工作。/她买了一个新手机。

Turn to page 159 for grammar reference.

LESSON 3

Communication activity

1 Work in groups of three. Interview each other about your lifestyles, using the questionnaire below.

生活方式问卷

1 你每天早上几点起床？

☐ 6—7点　☐ 7—9点　☐ 9—11点

2 你每星期做几个小时作业？

☐ 1小时以下　☐ 1—3小时　☐ 3小时以上

3 你每星期做几个小时运动？

☐ 2小时以下　☐ 2—5小时　☐ 5小时以上

4 你喜欢什么运动？ ______________

5 你在哪里复习准备考试？

☐ 图书馆　☐ 宿舍/家里　☐ 公园

6 你晚上通常做什么？ ______________

7 你周末喜欢做什么？ ______________

2 Report to the class, describing classmate(s) with similar and different lifestyles to yours.

Turn to pages 147 and 153 for more speaking practice.

Cultural corner

Planning ahead

Chinese culture has traditionally valued being well-prepared for the future. Chinese people like to make long-term plans for their lives and to be financially secure. Wary of spending too much, they like to save money for housing, children's education, and medical emergencies. Many parents also help their children with mortgages and wedding expenses. They often begin to put aside money when the child is just a baby.

But unlike Westerners, who usually book flights and hotels several months ahead, Chinese people often book only a month or so ahead at most. Most hotels accept on-the-spot bookings.

Character writing

These are two common radicals in Chinese. Do you know any other characters with the same radicals?

Radical	Meaning	Examples
灬	fire	点、照
心	heart	您、想

1 Look at the characters and identify the radicals.

然　　能　　怎　　意

2 Match the words with the meanings.

1 不好意思
2 开心
3 七点
4 照片

a photo
b 7 o'clock
c happy
d (something makes you feel) embarrassed

3 Trace the characters in the boxes.

心

意

点

照

Review and practice

1 Match the words with the meanings.

1 起床
2 吃饭
3 上课
4 做作业
5 写日记
6 睡觉

a do homework
b write a diary
c sleep
d have a meal
e get up
f attend a class

2 Write four sentences about what you did yesterday, using the words from Activity 1.

3 Answer the questions using your own information.

1 明年你多大？
2 你的中文作业要什么时候交给老师？
3 你打网球打得怎么样？
4 你打算去中国旅行吗？为什么？

4 Write two sentences to describe each picture, using the words below.

一边……一边……　　才
一……就……　　已经

a

b

Vocabulary extension

Match the words with the pictures.

1 shāngxīn 伤心	2 shēngqì 生气	3 kuàilè 快乐
4 chǎojià 吵架	5 xiào 笑	6 kū 哭

a

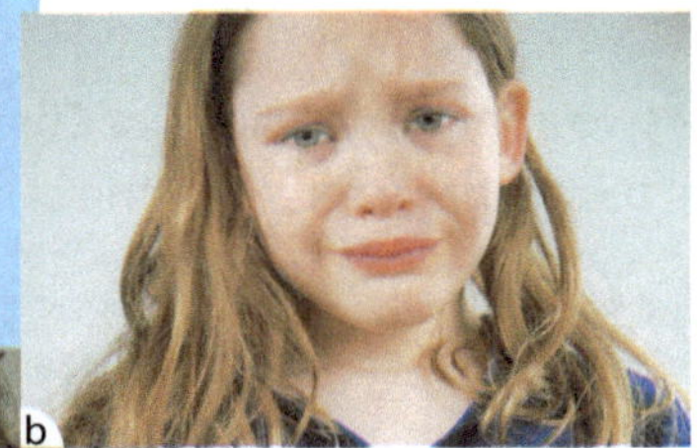
b

c

Now work in pairs. Ask and answer questions about what happened to you yesterday and how you felt.

Vocabulary review

Fill in the blanks.

____	běn	*measure word*	(used for books)
不好意思	bù hǎoyìsi		________
才	cái	*adv.*	not until
____	chídào	*v.*	be late
床	chuáng	*n.*	bed
得	de	*auxiliary word*	(used between a verb or an adjective and its complement to indicate result or degree)
读	dú	*v.*	________
放学	fàngxué	*v.*	school is over
复习	fùxí	*v.*	revise, review
故事	gùshi	*n.*	story
____	hái	*adv.*	still, yet, also
交	jiāo	*v.*	________
____	jiàoshì	*n.*	classroom
借	jiè	*v.*	________
就	jiù	*adv.*	exactly, as soon as
____	kāixīn	*adj.*	happy
考试	kǎoshì	*n.*	exam, test
____	kěnéng	*adj.*	possible
累	lèi	*adj.*	________
____	máng	*adj.*	busy
____	méi guānxi		it doesn't matter
难	nán	*adj.*	________
能	néng	*modal v.*	can
____	qǐchuáng	*v.*	get up
前	qián	*n.*	________

____	ràng	*v.*	let, allow, ask
____	rìjì	*n.*	diary
上床	shàngchuáng	*v.*	________
上课	shàngkè	*v.*	attend a class
睡觉	shuìjiào	*v.*	________
____	shuōhuà	*v.*	speak, talk
____	tiānqì	*n.*	weather
____	tóngxué	*n.*	classmate
图书馆	túshūguǎn	*n.*	________
完	wán	*v.*	complete
____	wèi shénme		why
下次	xiàcì	*n.*	next time
新闻	xīnwén	*n.*	news
一边	yìbiān	*adv.*	________
____	yǐjīng	*adv.*	already
因为	yīnwèi	*conj.*	________
用	yòng	*n./v.*	use
有趣	yǒuqù	*adj.*	________
早	zǎo	*adj.*	early
____	zhème	*pron.*	so, such
____	zhǔnbèi	*v.*	prepare
作业	zuòyè	*n.*	________
吵架	chǎojià	*v.*	argue
哭	kū	*v.*	cry
快乐	kuàilè	*adj.*	happy
伤心	shāngxīn	*adj.*	sad
生气	shēngqì	*adj.*	angry
笑	xiào	*v.*	laugh, smile

* The words in colour are not target words for the unit.

UNIT 2

Wǒ xǐhuan xià xuě tiān

我喜欢下雪天！

I love the snow!

LESSON | 1

Vocabulary and listening

11 **1 Work in pairs. Talk about what you can see in the picture. Use the words below to help you.**

chūntiān 春天	xiàtiān 夏天	qiūtiān 秋天	dōngtiān 冬天
màozi 帽子	wéijīn 围巾	shǒutào 手套	duǎnkù 短裤

Now listen and say the words.

12 **2 Work in pairs. Talk about which of the words below can be used to describe the weather in the picture from Activity 1.**

☐ lěng 冷	☐ nuǎnhuo 暖和	☐ xiàxuě 下雪
☐ rè 热	☐ liángshuǎng 凉爽	☐ xiàyǔ 下雨

Now listen and say the words.

13 **3 Mark, Amanda and Yeong-min are talking about what to wear while travelling. Listen to the conversation and answer the questions.**

1 他们要去什么地方玩？

2 那里的天气怎么样？

阿曼达：马克，你为什么穿这么多衣服？今天的天气很好，气温二十度。

马克：这里的天气比布里斯班的冷，我当然要多穿一些。

永民：那去西安旅行，你会穿什么衣服呢？听说西安冬天很冷，风很大，还会下雪。

阿曼达：我喜欢下雪天！

马克：下雪？我会多穿几件毛衣，戴围巾和手套，再带件大衣。

永民：穿这么多衣服，你还能走路吗？西安冬天的气温和首尔的差不多，我不打算带太多衣服。

阿曼达：成都的天气怎么样？和西安一样冷吗？

永民：成都没有西安那么冷。成都在南方，那里比北方暖和。

阿曼达：那么我可以穿我最喜欢的T恤和短裤，戴太阳镜了！

马克：我可以穿冲浪短裤！

永民：不行，不行！虽然成都没有西安那么冷，但是冬天的气温也在十度以下，你不能穿T恤和短裤。当然，如果你想看起来很酷，你可以戴墨镜。

New words

chuān	穿	wear (clothes)	shǒutào	手套	glove
qìwēn	气温	air temperature	zài	再	then, again
dù	度	degree	dài	带	bring, take
bǐ	比	than	chàbuduō	差不多	about the same
lěng	冷	cold	yíyàng	一样	the same
tīngshuō	听说	hear about	nuǎnhuo	暖和	nice and warm
dōngtiān	冬天	winter	duǎnkù	短裤	shorts
fēng	风	wind	tàiyáng	太阳	sun
dà	大	big, large	xíng	行	be all right
xiàxuě	下雪	snow	suīrán	虽然	although
máoyī	毛衣	sweater, jumper	rúguǒ	如果	if
dài	戴	wear (clothing accessories like hat, scarf, etc.)	mòjìng	墨镜	sunglasses
wéijīn	围巾	scarf			

13

4 Listen again and check the clothes they can wear on their trip.

☐ a 毛衣　☐ b 围巾
☐ c 手套　☐ d 大衣
☐ e T恤　☐ f 短裤

5 Work in groups of three. Look at the photo and talk about the weather and clothes you could wear.

Pronunciation and speaking

Difference between "c" and "ch"

14

1 Check the correct initials for the underlined characters.

1 成都	☐ c	☐ ch
2 冲浪	☐ c	☐ ch
3 下次	☐ c	☐ ch
4 吃饭	☐ c	☐ ch

Now listen and repeat.

15

2 Say the sentences aloud.

1 Wǒmen kěyǐ xiàcì yìqǐ chī Hánguó cài
我们 可以 下次 一起 吃 韩国 菜。

2 Chéngdū de chuāncài hěn hǎochī
成都 的 川菜 很 好吃。

3 Wǒ shíyī diǎn cái shàngchuáng shuìjiào
我 十一 点 才 上床 睡觉 。

4 Dōngtiān qù Sìchuān bù néng chuān duǎnkù
冬天 去 四川 不 能 穿 短裤 。

5 Wǒmen kěyǐ zuò chuán cānguān jǐngdiǎn
我们 可以 坐 船 参观 景点 。

Now listen and repeat.

16

3 Listen and say the words.

1	tiānqì 天气	lěng 冷	nuǎnhuo 暖和	dōngtiān 冬天
2	duǎnkù 短裤	máoyī 毛衣	wéijīn 围巾	shǒutào 手套
3	qìwēn 气温	chuān 穿	dài 戴	mòjìng 墨镜

4 Write down information about your most recent leisure travel, including the time, place, season, weather and the clothes you wore.

Now work in pairs. Ask and answer questions about each other's travel experiences.

CHINESE TO GO

17

Talking about the weather

Dòng sǐ le
冻死了！ It's freezing!

Yǔ zhēn dà
雨真大！ It's pouring with rain!

Bié wàng le dài sǎn
别忘了带伞。 Don't forget to bring an umbrella.

Guāfēng le
刮风了。 It's windy.

LESSON 2

Reading and writing

1 Match the weather words with their symbols.

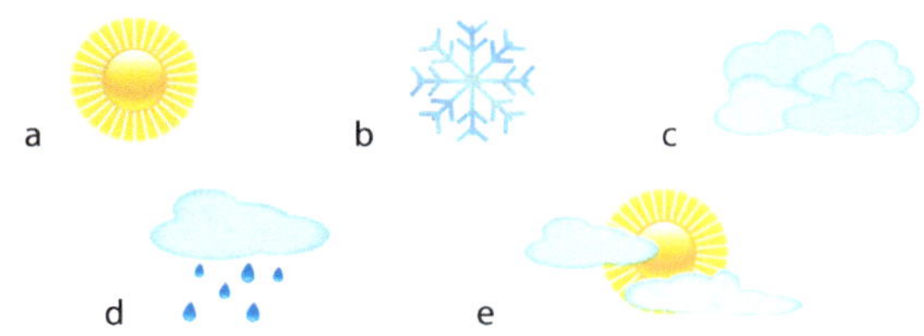

1 qíng 晴　2 yīn 阴　3 duōyún 多云　4 yǔ 雨　5 xuě 雪

18

2 Read the online weather reports for Xi'an and Chengdu, and check the true statements.

- ☐ 1 冷空气下个星期只会影响北方地区。
- ☐ 2 白天和夜间的气温都会下降10℃。
- ☐ 3 西北和西南一些地方降温更多。

New words

yùbào 预报	forecast	yèjiān 夜间	nighttime
qǐ 起	begin, start	chābié 差别	difference
kōngqì 空气	air	dádào 达到	reach
jiāng 将	will, shall	yǐshàng 以上	above
yǐngxiǎng 影响	affect, influence	duōyún 多云	cloudy
bùfen 部分	part	zhuǎn 转	turn, change
dìqū 地区	area	qíng 晴	sunny
shòu 受	suffer, be subjected to	yīn 阴	overcast
xiàjiàng 下降	descend, fall	xiǎo 小	small, little
báitiān 白天	daytime	yǔ 雨	rain

天气预报

从下个星期起，冷空气将影响我国大部分地区。受冷空气的影响，北方的气温将下降4~8℃，很多地方白天和夜间的气温差别将达到10℃，西北和西南一些地方的温差将在15℃以上。

西安

日期	二月七日 星期一	二月八日 星期二	二月九日 星期三
天气	多云转晴	多云转阴	大雪
气温	–4℃/1℃	–5℃/2℃	–6℃/1℃

成都

日期	二月七日 星期一	二月八日 星期二	二月九日 星期三
天气	晴	多云转阴	小雨
气温	1℃/7℃	0℃/6℃	–2℃/6℃

3 **Read again and check the correct words to complete the sentences.**

1 西安二月八日的气温是 ______。

☐ a 0℃～6℃ ☐ b −5℃～2℃

2 成都星期一的气温是 ______。

☐ a −4℃～1℃ ☐ b 1℃～7℃

3 下个星期三西安会 ______。

☐ a 下大雪 ☐ b 下小雨

4 二月七日成都的天气是 ______。

☐ a 晴 ☐ b 多云转晴

19

4 **Listen and match the letters of the cities to the correct places on the map.**

a	Běijīng 北京	c	Xī'ān 西安	e	Guǎngzhōu 广州
b	Shànghǎi 上海	d	Chéngdū 成都	f	Xiānggǎng 香港

20

Now listen and put the weather symbols from Activity 1 in the correct places on the map.

5 **Think of a destination you would like to travel to. Describe what the weather would be like and the clothes and other items you would need to bring.**

Language in use

Describing similarity using A 和 B + 差不多/一样

1 **Look at the sentences.**

A	和	B	Adjective	Complement
西安冬天的气温	和	首尔的（气温）	差不多。	
他的工作	和	我的（工作）	差不多。	
我的看法	和	你的（看法）	一样。	
王玉	和	阿曼达	一样	高。

Now check the two correct explanations.

☐ 1 和 is used to connect A and B to describe similarity.

☐ 2 差不多 means "the same", while 一样 means "about the same".

☐ 3 A complement can be used after 一样, while 差不多 often stands alone.

2 **Write the sentences in Chinese.**

1 The weather next week will be similar to the weather this week.

2 The length of the journey by bus is similar to the length of the journey by train.

3 Is the winter in London as cold as the winter in Beijing?

4 Are you as tall as her?

Making comparisons using A 比/没有 B + adjective

1 Look at the sentences.

A	比/没有	B	Adjective
这里的天气	比	布里斯班的（天气）	冷。
布里斯班的天气	没有	这里的（天气）	冷。
南方	比	北方	暖和。
北方	没有	南方	暖和。
你	比	她	高。
她	没有	你	高。

Now check the two correct explanations.

☐ 1 比 is used to show that A is higher in degree than B in terms of the adjective used.

☐ 2 没有 is used to show that A is higher in degree than B in terms of the adjective used.

☐ 3 When the same head noun exists in both A and B, the second head noun can be omitted.

2 Rewrite the sentences using 没有.

1 西安的冬天比成都冷。
2 北方的温差比南方大。
3 今天比昨天暖和。
4 这件大衣比那件大衣漂亮。

Describing future actions with 要/会

1 Look at the sentences.

Adverbial of time	Subject	Modal verb	Verb phrase
晚上	我	要	准备星期三的考试。
明天	我	要	交作业。
	你	会	穿什么衣服呢？
周末	我	不会	去公园。

Now check the two correct explanations.

☐ 1 要 is used to describe future actions, indicating the need or intention of the subject or doer.

☐ 2 会 is used to describe future actions, showing a high probability.

☐ 3 要 and 会 can be used after a verb when describing future actions.

2 Complete the sentences using 要 or 会.

1 今年冬天我不 ______ 去韩国旅行。
2 下周一考试，所以这周末我 ______ 复习准备考试。
3 今天晚上王玉 ______ 上课，所以她不 ______ 和我们一起去看电影。

▶ Turn to page 160 for grammar reference.

LESSON | 3

Communication activity

1 **Write two true statements and one false statement about yourself and the weather. For example,**

我每年冬天都去韩国玩。
我喜欢滑雪。
我去韩国的时候穿T恤和短裤。

Now work in pairs. Listen to your partner's statements, and guess which statement is false.

2 **Explain the reasons for your guess. Use the following expressions where appropriate.**

我觉得……，因为……

Turn to pages 147 and 153 for more speaking practice.

Cultural corner

From freezing snow to tropical forest

As one of the largest countries in the world, China covers a vast territory, and different parts of the country have very different weather conditions, from the freezing winters of the north-east, to the tropical climate of Hainan in the south, and the arid deserts of the west.

Such differences in the weather naturally influence the lifestyles of people in the different regions, affecting what food grows locally and appears in local cuisine, and shaping regional customs. Even a stranger can be sure of a warm welcome and a hot drink in Harbin, where exposure to the cold can have serious consequences. In tropical parts of Yunnan, the annual Water-Splashing Festival lets you celebrate the new year of the Dai ethnic group and keep cool at the same time.

Character writing

These are two common radicals in Chinese. Do you know any other characters with the same radicals?

Radical	Meaning	Examples
囗	enclosure	国、园
冫	ice	冲、冰

1 **Look at the characters and identify the radicals.**

围　冷　回　次

2 **Match the words with the meanings.**

1 围巾　　a next time
2 回家　　b very cold
3 很冷　　c scarf
4 下次　　d go home

3 **Trace the characters in the boxes.**

Review and practice

1 **Match the words with the meanings.**

1 天气　　a air temperature
2 暖和　　b air
3 差别　　c weather
4 气温　　d difference
5 空气　　e nice and warm

2 **Write three sentences about the weather in your area. Compare it with another place you know, using A 比/没有 B + adjective.**

3 **Write three sentences about a friend, explaining your similarities by using A 和 B + 差不多/一样.**

4 **Write two sentences to describe each picture.**

a

b

Vocabulary extension

Match the words with the pictures.

1 雨伞 yǔsǎn	2 雨鞋 yǔxié	3 羽绒服 yǔróngfú
4 连衣裙 liányīqún	5 夹克 jiākè	6 牛仔裤 niúzǎikù

Now work in pairs. Discuss in what season or weather you would wear or use these things.

a b c

Vocabulary review

Fill in the blanks.

白天	báitiān	*n.*	daytime
______	bǐ	*prep.*	than
部分	bùfen	*n.*	______
差别	chābié	*n.*	difference
差不多	chàbuduō	*adj.*	______
______	chuān	*v.*	wear (clothes)
达到	dádào	*v.*	______
______	dà	*adj.*	big, large
带	dài	*v.*	bring, take
戴	dài	*v.*	wear (clothing accessories like hat, scarf, etc.)
地区	dìqū	*n.*	area
______	dōngtiān	*n.*	winter
度	dù	*n.*	______
短裤	duǎnkù	*n.*	shorts
多云	duōyún	*n.*	______
______	fēng	*n.*	wind
将	jiāng	*adv.*	will, shall
______	kōngqì	*n.*	air
冷	lěng	*adj.*	cold
______	máoyī	*n.*	sweater, jumper
墨镜	mòjìng	*n.*	______
______	nuǎnhuo	*adj.*	nice and warm
起	qǐ	*v.*	begin, start
气温	qìwēn	*n.*	______
______	qíng	*adj.*	sunny
如果	rúguǒ	*conj.*	if
手套	shǒutào	*n.*	______
受	shòu	*v.*	suffer, be subjected to
虽然	suīrán	*conj.*	______

______	tàiyáng	*n.*	sun
听说	tīngshuō	*v.*	______
围巾	wéijīn	*n.*	scarf
下降	xiàjiàng	*v.*	______
______	xiàxuě	*v.*	snow
小	xiǎo	*adj.*	______
行	xíng	*v.*	be all right
夜间	yèjiān	*n.*	______
______	yíyàng	*adj.*	the same
以上	yǐshàng	*n.*	above
阴	yīn	*adj.*	______
影响	yǐngxiǎng	*v./n.*	affect, influence
______	yǔ	*n.*	rain
预报	yùbào	*n./v.*	forecast
______	zài	*adv.*	then, again
转	zhuǎn	*v.*	turn, change
春天	chūntiān	*n.*	spring
夹克	jiākè	*n.*	jacket
连衣裙	liányīqún	*n.*	one-piece dress
凉爽	liángshuǎng	*adj.*	cool
帽子	màozi	*n.*	hat
牛仔裤	niúzǎikù	*n.*	jeans
秋天	qiūtiān	*n.*	autumn
热	rè	*adj.*	hot
夏天	xiàtiān	*n.*	summer
羽绒服	yǔróngfú	*n.*	down garment
雨伞	yǔsǎn	*n.*	umbrella
雨鞋	yǔxié	*n.*	rain boot

UNIT 3

Xīnnián hǎo
新年好！

Happy New Year!

LESSON 1

Vocabulary and listening

21

1 Match the words with the pictures.

chá	tángguǒ	hóngbāo	shuǐguǒ
1 茶	2 糖果	3 红包	4 水果

Now listen and say the words.

22

2 Work in pairs. Label the rooms of the house with the words.

kètīng	chúfáng	wèishēngjiān
1 客厅	2 厨房	3 卫生间
cāntīng	wòshì	
4 餐厅	5 卧室	

Now listen and say the words.

23

3 Amanda, Steve and Yeong-min are visiting Wang Yu and her family. Listen to the conversation and answer the questions.

1 阿曼达他们为什么去王玉的家？
2 王玉的家怎么样？有几间卧室？

阿曼达： 王玉，新年好！
王玉： 新年好！请进，请进。爸爸、妈妈，我的朋友们来了。我给你们介绍一下。这是我爸爸、妈妈。这是我的朋友阿曼达、永民和史蒂夫。
阿曼达等人： 叔叔、阿姨，新年好！
王玉的爸爸： 新年好！这是给你们的红包。
阿曼达等人： 谢谢叔叔阿姨。
王玉的妈妈： 快请坐。请吃糖，还有水果。你们想喝茶还是果汁？
阿曼达： 我想喝果汁。
史蒂夫和永民： 我喝茶。
永民： 你家地方很大，也很漂亮。
王玉： 我带你们参观一下我家。这是客厅，旁边是餐厅。

史蒂夫：你家有几间卧室？
王玉：三间。这是我哥哥的房间，对面是卫生间。
阿曼达：这是谁的房间？
王玉：这是我和姐姐的房间。我爸爸妈妈的房间在对面。
永民：什么这么香？
王玉：我妈妈正在做她的拿手菜——糖醋鱼。我带你们去厨房看看，好吗？
阿曼达和史蒂夫：太好了！

New words

jìn 进	enter, come in	pángbiān 旁边	next to, beside
jièshào 介绍	introduce	cāntīng 餐厅	dining room
shūshu 叔叔	uncle	jiān 间	(used for smallest units of housing)
āyí 阿姨	aunt	wòshì 卧室	bedroom
hóngbāo 红包	red packet (money wrapped in red paper as a gift)	duìmiàn 对面	opposite side
táng 糖	sugar, sweet	wèishēngjiān 卫生间	toilet
shuǐguǒ 水果	fruit	xiāng 香	savoury, fragrant
hē 喝	drink	zhèngzài 正在	in the process of
chá 茶	tea	náshǒucài 拿手菜	signature dish
guǒzhī 果汁	fruit juice	tángcùyú 糖醋鱼	fish in sweet-and-sour sauce
kètīng 客厅	living room		

23

4 Listen again and label the rooms of Wang Yu's house with the words.

1 客厅　2 餐厅　3 卫生间　4 哥哥的卧室
5 爸爸妈妈的卧室　6 她和姐姐的卧室

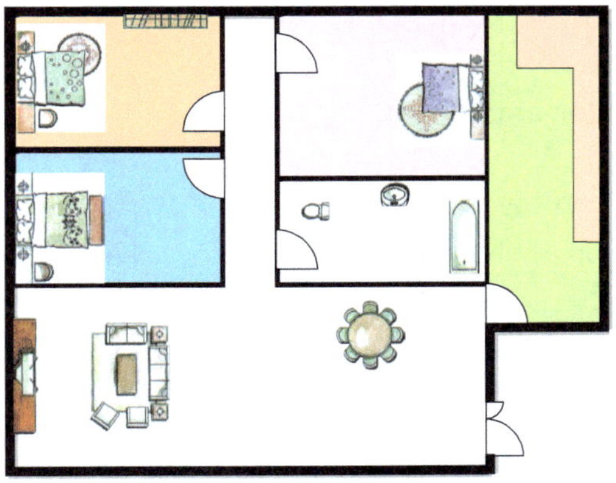

5 Write several sentences to describe your home. Start with:

我家有……间卧室，客厅在……

6 Work in pairs. Take turns to read your sentences to your partner, who will draw a floor plan of your house.

Now check and see if your partner's floor plan is correct.

Pronunciation and speaking

Difference between "uo" and "e"

24

1 Check the correct finals for the underlined characters.

1 请坐	☐ uo	☐ e
2 喝茶	☐ uo	☐ e
3 果汁	☐ uo	☐ e
4 客厅	☐ uo	☐ e
5 这么	☐ uo	☐ e
6 过年	☐ uo	☐ e

Now listen and repeat.

25

2 Read the sentences aloud.

Wǒ gēge qùguo Měiguó
1 我哥哥去过 美国。

Hěn duō rén xǐhuan hē guǒzhī
2 很 多 人 喜欢 喝 果汁。

Nǐ juéde Yīngguó zěnmeyàng
3 你 觉得 英国 怎么样 ？

Tā zuò zài kètīng li děng gēge
4 他 坐 在 客厅 里 等 哥哥。

Wǒmen zuò huǒchē háishi zuò fēijī qù Hánguó
5 我们 坐 火车 还是 坐 飞机 去 韩国？

Now listen and repeat.

26

3 Listen and say the words.

1	xīnnián 新年	hóngbāo 红包	qǐng zuò 请 坐	hē chá 喝 茶
2	shuǐguǒ 水果	táng 糖	guǒzhī 果汁	náshǒucài 拿手菜
3	kètīng 客厅	cāntīng 餐厅	wòshì 卧室	wèishēngjiān 卫生间

4 Work in pairs.

A: You are a Chinese host entertaining some visitors during Chinese New Year.

B: You are paying a New Year visit to A's home.

Now change roles.

CHINESE TO GO

27

Expressions used at New Year celebrations

Gōngxǐ-fācái 恭喜发财。	May you be prosperous.
Wànshì-rúyì 万事如意。	May everything go as you hope.
Gěi nǐ yāsuìqián 给 你 压岁钱。	Here's your Chinese New Year gift money.
Wǒ jìng nǐ yì bēi 我 敬 你 一 杯。	I'd like to propose a toast to you.
Gānbēi 干杯！	Cheers!

LESSON 2

Reading and writing

1 Complete the phrases with the correct verbs.

guà 挂	tiē 贴	wán 玩	chàng 唱	bài 拜	gěi 给

1 ______ chūnlián 春联　　2 ______ yóuxì 游戏

3 ______ nián 年　　4 ______ hóngbāo 红包

5 ______ gē 歌　　6 ______ dēnglong 灯笼

28

2 Read Steve's article about Chinese New Year in the school magazine.

New words

Chūnjié 春节	Spring Festival, Chinese New Year
tuányuán 团圆	have a reunion
jiérì 节日	festival
tiē 贴	paste
chūnlián 春联	Spring Festival couplets
guà 挂	hang up
dēnglong 灯笼	lantern
qìngzhù 庆祝	celebrate
chúxī 除夕	Chinese New Year's Eve
cānjiā 参加	participate in, take part in
yòu 又	also
wán 玩	play
yóuxì 游戏	game
dànián chūyī 大年初一	Chinese New Year's Day
bàinián 拜年	pay a New Year visit
xiān 先	first
bāo 包	wrap
jiǎozi 饺子	dumpling
rènao 热闹	bustling

过年了！

作者：史蒂夫

今年我在中国过春节了！春节也就是中国人的新年，是家人团圆的节日。很多人家的门口都会贴春联，挂红灯笼，庆祝新年的到来。

除夕夜，我参加了学校的除夕派对。很多同学都没有回家，都在北京过春节。我们又玩游戏又唱歌，大家都玩得很开心。

大年初一，很多人很早就起床了，去朋友家拜年。中午我和永民、阿曼达去王玉家拜年。我们先一起包饺子，然后吃饭。王玉的妈妈准备了很多菜，我最喜欢吃的菜是糖醋鱼。

我觉得中国的春节又热闹又好玩儿。

3 Choose the correct answers to the questions.

1 What is the first paragraph mainly about?

☐ a 红灯笼　☐ b 春节　☐ c 春联

2 What is the second paragraph mainly about?

☐ a 除夕派对　☐ b 同学　☐ c 玩游戏

3 What is the main subject of the third paragraph?

☐ a 包饺子　☐ b 吃饭　☐ c 拜年

4 Read again and answer the questions.

1 除夕夜史蒂夫去了哪里？做了什么？
2 中国人在哪里贴春联，挂红灯笼？
3 史蒂夫他们为什么大年初一去王玉家？
4 他们在王玉家做了什么？
5 史蒂夫最喜欢吃什么菜？
6 史蒂夫觉得中国的春节怎么样？

5 Complete the description of the most important festival in your country.

在我的国家，最重要（zhòngyào）（important）的节日是______。这个节日是_____月_____日。

这一天，我们会________。

我们先____________，然后____________。我最喜欢__________。

我觉得这个节日又__________又__________。

Language in use

Describing actions in progress using 正在

1 Look at the sentences.

Adverbial	Subject	正在	Verb phrase
	我妈妈	正在	做她的拿手菜。
老师进来的时候，	同学们	正在	看书。
你打电话的时候，	王玉	正（在）	包饺子。
昨天下午三点，	他们	（正）在	玩游戏。

Now check the two correct explanations.

☐ 1 正在 is used to indicate an action in progress at a specific time or during a certain period of time.

☐ 2 正在 is only used for actions happening in the present.

☐ 3 Either 正 or 在 can be omitted if the emphasis is not on the action happening at a specific time.

2 Write the sentences in Chinese.

1 They are playing football at the sports ground.
2 I was watching TV at 8 o'clock yesterday evening.
3 She was attending class when you called.
4 At 4 o'clock every afternoon, Mark goes jogging.

Expressing "both… and…" with 又……又……

1 Look at the sentences.

First condition/quality	Second condition/quality
我们玩游戏。	我们唱歌。
我们又玩游戏又唱歌。	
他们贴春联。	他们挂红灯笼。
他们又贴春联又挂红灯笼。	
中国的春节很热闹。	中国的春节很好玩儿。
中国的春节又热闹又好玩儿。	
他很高。	他很帅。
他又高又帅。	
王玉的家很大。	王玉的家很漂亮。
王玉的家又大又漂亮。	

Now check the two correct explanations.

☐ 1 又……又…… is used to decribe conditions or qualities that occur one after the other.

☐ 2 又……又…… is used to connect two verb phrases or adjectives as the predicate.

☐ 3 The phrases connected by 又……又…… must be of the same structure or part of speech.

2 Join the sentences together using 又……又…….

1 他们唱歌。/他们跳舞。
2 中国菜很好吃。/中国菜很便宜。
3 坐火车很快。/坐火车很方便。

Describing sequences with 先……然后……

1 Look at the sentences.

First event/action	Second event/action
我们先一起包饺子，	然后(我们)吃饭。
我们先去西安，	然后(我们)去成都。
他们先喝茶，	然后参观王玉的家。
王玉先吃晚饭，	然后看电影。

Now check the two correct explanations.

☐ 1 先……然后…… is used to connect two actions or events that happen at the same time.

☐ 2 先 must be placed between the subject and the verb of the first event, while 然后 is usually put at the beginning of the clause stating the second event.

☐ 3 If the subjects of the verb phrases connected by 先……然后…… are the same, the second subject is usually omitted.

2 Join the sentences together using 先……然后…….

1 安娜看书。/安娜打篮球。
2 永民跟老师见面。/永民吃饭。
3 马克看电影。/马克去同学的生日派对。

Turn to page 161 for grammar reference.

LESSON 3

Communication activity

1 **Work in groups of four. You are planning a New Year party. The theme is "China". Create a party plan. Think about:**

Theme	中国
Time and place	
Decorations	
Costumes	
Games and activities	
Food and drink	

2 **Share your party plan with another group.**

Turn to pages 148 and 154 for more speaking practice.

Cultural corner

Being a guest in China

When invited to a Chinese household, a guest can typically expect a sumptuous meal prepared by the host. Although the meal will be carefully prepared and the quantity more than enough, the host will probably say, "I'm afraid it's not much. I hope you don't mind." During the meal, the host will serve food and drink all the time. They want to make sure the guests always have some food on their plates. Some guests will leave some food uneaten to suggest that they are so full that they cannot eat any more.

Good gifts to bring to a Chinese household include fruit, wine and tea. The choice of gifts one should bring depends on the relationship between the guest and host. If they are friends, fruit makes a good gift. If the host is older than the guest, the guest may bring wine or tea, or a small present which comes from his/her country as a token to express thanks for being invited.

Character writing

These are two common radicals in Chinese. Do you know any other characters with the same radicals?

Radical	Meaning	Examples
艹	grass, plant	菜、英
广	big room, space	床、应

1 Look at the characters and identify the radicals.

茶　节　店　庆

2 Match the words with the meanings.

1 庆祝	a Spring Festival
2 喝茶	b get up
3 起床	c celebrate
4 春节	d drink tea

3 Trace the characters in the boxes.

节

茶

庆

床

Review and practice

1 Circle the odd word out in each line.

1 饺子　糖醋鱼　挂
2 对面　节日　旁边
3 拜年　春联　灯笼
4 热闹　团圆　参加
5 挂　贴　游戏

2 Answer the questions using 正在.

1 昨天下午四点你在做什么？
2 今天早上八点你在做什么？
3 你上课的时候，你的家人正在做什么？

3 Complete the paragraph using appropriate words.

今天是安娜的生日。早上七点，安娜 ______ 起床了。她 ______ 学中文，______ 去打篮球。晚上六点是安娜的生日派对。朋友们 ______ 跳舞 ______ 唱歌。大家 ______ 很高兴。

4 Write two sentences to describe the picture, using 又……又…… and 正在.

Vocabulary extension

Match the words with the different fruits in the picture.

1 橙子 chéngzi	2 梨 lí	3 香蕉 xiāngjiāo
4 苹果 píngguǒ	5 葡萄 pútao	6 西瓜 xīguā

Now work in pairs. Ask and answer questions about what fruit you like.

A: 你喜欢吃水果吗？你最喜欢什么水果？

B: 我喜欢吃水果，我最喜欢……

Vocabulary review

Fill in the blanks.

阿姨	āyí	*n.*	aunt
拜年	bàinián	*v.*	_____
_____	bāo	*v.*	wrap
参加	cānjiā	*v.*	_____
餐厅	cāntīng	*n.*	dining room
_____	chá	*n.*	tea
除夕	chúxī	*n.*	Chinese New Year's Eve
春节	Chūnjié	*n.*	_____
春联	chūnlián	*n.*	Spring Festival couplets
大年初一	dànián chūyī		Chinese New Year's Day
灯笼	dēnglong	*n.*	lantern
_____	duìmiàn	*n.*	opposite side
挂	guà	*v.*	_____
果汁	guǒzhī	*n.*	fruit juice
_____	hē	*v.*	drink
红包	hóngbāo	*n.*	red packet (money wrapped in red paper as a gift)
间	jiān	*measure word*	(used for smallest units of housing)
饺子	jiǎozi	*n.*	dumpling
节日	jiérì	*n.*	_____
_____	jièshào	*v.*	introduce
_____	jìn	*v.*	enter, come in
客厅	kètīng	*n.*	living room
拿手菜	náshǒucài	*n.*	_____
_____	pángbiān	*n.*	next to, beside
庆祝	qìngzhù	*v.*	_____
_____	rènao	*adj.*	bustling
叔叔	shūshu	*n.*	_____
_____	shuǐguǒ	*n.*	fruit
糖	táng	*n.*	_____
糖醋鱼	tángcùyú	*n.*	_____
贴	tiē	*v.*	_____
团圆	tuányuán	*v.*	have a reunion
_____	wán	*v.*	play
卫生间	wèishēngjiān	*n.*	_____
卧室	wòshì	*n.*	bedroom
_____	xiān	*adv.*	first
香	xiāng	*adj.*	savoury, fragrant
游戏	yóuxì	*n.*	_____
又	yòu	*adv.*	also
_____	zhèngzài	*adv.*	in the process of
橙子	chéngzi	*n.*	orange
梨	lí	*n.*	pear
苹果	píngguǒ	*n.*	apple
葡萄	pútao	*n.*	grape
西瓜	xīguā	*n.*	watermelon
香蕉	xiāngjiāo	*n.*	banana

UNIT 4

Wǒmen zěnme qù ne
我们怎么去呢？

How do we get there?

LESSON 1

Vocabulary and listening

29

1 Match the words with the signs.

1 shì zhōngxīn 市 中心　2 chūzūchēzhàn 出租车 站

3 bīnguǎn 宾馆　4 gōnggòng qìchēzhàn 公共 汽车站

Now listen and say the words.

30

2 Listen and complete the signs.

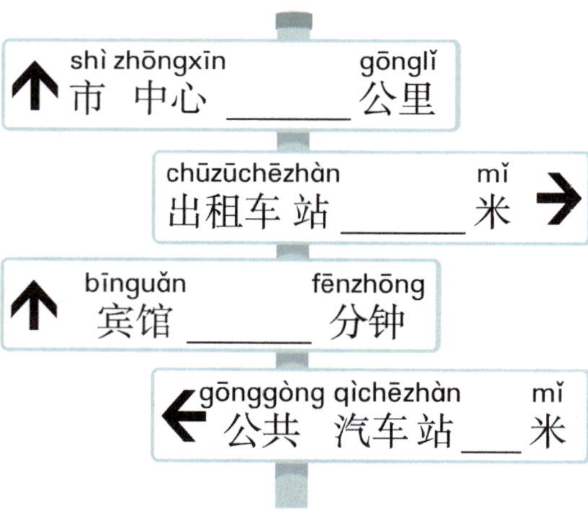

31

3 Mark, Amanda and Yeong-min have arrived in Xi'an. Listen to the conversation and answer the questions.

1 他们为什么要问路？
2 他们想去哪些地方？
3 西安有什么好玩儿的地方？

永民：坐高铁真快，才五个多小时就到西安了！现在我们怎么去古城宾馆呢？

马克：古城宾馆应该在钟楼附近，咱们到外面问问人吧。……请问，从这里到钟楼怎么走？有多远？

路人：钟楼在市中心，离这里很近，差不多五公里，坐出租车十分钟就到了。

马克：请问出租车站在哪里？

路人：往前走五十米，再向右拐，你就可以看到出租车站了。

阿曼达：谢谢您。那您知道从市中心怎么去古城墙和兵马俑吗？

路人：古城墙在市中心南边，走路就可以到。兵马俑很远，在西安市东边三十公里，你们可以坐出租车或者地铁去。

永民：西安还有什么好玩儿的地方吗？

路人：你们应该去大雁塔，它在西安市的南边。

马克：大雁塔看起来像大雁吗？哈哈……

永民：马克，别开玩笑了。

阿曼达：大清真寺呢？

路人：那里也应该去。大清真寺在钟楼附近，很容易找！

阿曼达：我知道了。太谢谢您了。

路人：不客气。祝你们在西安玩得开心！再见。

New words

gāo tiě 高铁	high-speed train	qiáng 墙	wall
gǔ 古	ancient, old	zǒulù 走路	walk
bīnguǎn 宾馆	hotel	xiàng 像	look like
zánmen 咱们	we, us	kāi wánxiào 开 玩笑	make a joke
wàimiàn 外面	outside	róngyì 容易	easy
gōnglǐ 公里	kilometre	zhǎo 找	look for
xiàng 向	to, towards	bú kèqi 不客气	you're welcome
yòu 右	the right side	zhù 祝	wish
guǎi 拐	turn	zàijiàn 再见	goodbye
nín 您	you (respectful form)		

31

4 **Listen again and mark the correct locations of the following places on the map.**

1 Zhōnglóu 钟楼　2 Gǔchéngqiáng 古城墙　3 Dàyàntǎ 大雁塔

4 Qīngzhēnsì 清真寺　5 Bīngmǎyǒng 兵马俑

5 **Work in pairs. Ask and answer questions about**

- how far away the following places are;
- how to get to these places from where you are now.

Use the conversation in Activity 3 to help you.

洗手间　地铁站

图书馆　公共汽车站

Pronunciation and speaking

The initials: "zh", "ch", "sh"

32

1 Check the correct initials for the underlined characters.

1 城市 ☐ zh ☐ ch ☐ sh
2 中心 ☐ zh ☐ ch ☐ sh
3 这里 ☐ zh ☐ ch ☐ sh
4 差不多 ☐ zh ☐ ch ☐ sh
5 出租车 ☐ zh ☐ ch ☐ sh
6 十分钟 ☐ zh ☐ ch ☐ sh

Now listen and repeat.

33

2 Say the sentences aloud.

Wǒ zài zhège shāngdiàn mǎile yí gè shǒujī
1 我在这个商店买了一个手机。

Shūdiàn de shòuhuòyuán wèn wǒ de shēngrì
2 书店的售货员问我的生日。

Zhège shǔjià wǒ qù Zhōngguó zuò zhìyuànzhě
3 这个暑假我去中国做志愿者。

Nǐ rènshi zài chāoshì shàngbān de rén ma
4 你认识在超市上班的人吗？

Now listen and repeat.

34

3 Listen and say the words.

	fēijīchǎng	huǒchēzhàn	shì zhōngxīn
1	飞机场	火车站	市中心
	zěnme zǒu	wǎng qián zǒu	xiàng yòu guǎi
2	怎么走	往前走	向右拐
	duō yuǎn	fùjìn	róngyì
3	多远	附近	容易
	wǔshí mǐ	zuǒyòu	chàbuduō
4	五十米	左右	差不多

4 Write down information about how to get to the following places from your current location, including the means of transport, the time required and the cost.

huǒchēzhàn 火车站　　fēijīchǎng 飞机场

shì zhōngxīn 市中心　　zuì jìn de shūdiàn 最近的书店

Now work in pairs. Ask and answer questions about how to get to these places.

CHINESE TO GO

35

Asking for repetition and clarification

Wǒ méi tīng qīngchu 我没听清楚。	I didn't catch that.
Qǐng zài shuō yí biàn 请再说一遍。	Please say that again.
Nǐ míngbai ma 你明白吗？	Do you understand?
Wǒ bù míngbai 我不明白。	I don't understand.
Nín shì shuō 您是说……？	Do you mean…?

LESSON 2

Reading and writing

1 **Work in pairs. Talk about your journey to class every day, using the words in the box. Say**

- how far away your home is;
- how long the journey takes;
- how you travel;
- what time you leave and arrive.

kāi chē 开车 drive a vehicle	jìnrù 进入 enter
líkāi 离开 leave, exit	dàodá 到达 arrive
shàng xià chē 上/下车 get on/off a vehicle	

36

2 **Read the travel guide about Xi'an and answer the questions.**

1 去秦始皇兵马俑博物馆，可以坐什么车？
2 坐什么车又快又方便？
3 坐什么车比较慢？

请问，到了西安，怎么去秦始皇兵马俑博物馆？

106个回答 · 2268关注

西安人

欢迎来西安玩！

去秦始皇兵马俑博物馆，你可以坐出租车或开车，也可以坐地铁或火车。

坐出租车或者开车又快又方便。如果不堵车，从西安市中心到高速公路只要十五分钟左右。在高速公路上开三十公里以后，进入临潼。离开高速公路以后，再开大约十分钟，就到秦始皇兵马俑博物馆了。出租车车费大约一百八十元。

坐地铁也很方便。你需要找到离你最近的地铁站，换乘到9号线，在“华清池”站下车，再换乘公交车“临潼游613路”，就可以到达“秦俑村”了。不过，如果你换乘地铁的次数比较多，就比较慢。

另外，你也可以从西安火车站坐火车到临潼，只需要二十多分钟；到了临潼火车站以后，也要换乘“临潼游613路”，不过从临潼火车站到“秦俑村”，比从“华清池”站要远。

祝你玩得愉快！

New words

bówùguǎn 博物馆	museum	líkāi 离开	leave, exit	lù 路	bus route
kāi 开	drive (a vehicle)	chēfèi 车费	(passenger) fare	gōngjiāo 公交	public transport
kuài 快	fast	dàyuē 大约	approximately	dào dá 到达	arrive
dǔchē 堵车	be stuck/caught in traffic	yuán 元	yuan, Chinese currency unit	búguò 不过	however, but
gāosù gōnglù 高速公路	motorway, freeway	huàn chéng 换乘	transfer	bǐjiào 比较	comparatively
jìnrù 进入	enter	xiàn 线	line	màn 慢	slow

3 **Read again and complete the table.**

	时间	价钱
出租车		
公共汽车		
火车		

Now work in pairs. Say which way you'd prefer to travel and why.

4 **A friend is travelling by train to visit you. Write him/her an email explaining how to get to your home from the railway station.**

Language in use

Talking about distance using 离/多远

1 **Look at the sentences.**

Topic			Comment
A	离	B	
伦敦	离	香港	多远?
伦敦	离	香港	9000多公里。
钟楼	离	这里	多远?
钟楼	离	这里	很近。
火车站	（离）	（这里）	多远?
			不远。

Now check the two correct explanations.

☐ 1 离 is used to introduce the starting point of a distance between two places.

☐ 2 多远 is used to ask about how far away one place is from another.

☐ 3 离 and 这里 can be left out if the starting point is obviously known in the context.

2 **Write questions about the underlined parts of the sentences.**

1 北京离成都<u>不远</u>。

2 北京离上海大约有<u>1200公里</u>。

3 图书馆离这里<u>很近</u>。

Describing distance using 从A到B

1 Look at the sentences.

Topic				Comment	
从	A	到	B	Verb phrase	Duration
从	这里	到	钟楼，	坐出租车	十分钟就到了。
从	市中心	到	兵马俑，	坐公共汽车	要一个小时。
从	市中心	到	高速公路，	开车	要十五分钟左右。
从	宿舍	到	超市，	走路	大约五分钟。

Now check the two correct explanations.

☐ 1 从 is used before A to indicate the starting point, while 到 is used before B, indicating the ending point.

☐ 2 The verb phrase for means of transport can be used after the duration.

☐ 3 The verb phrase for means of transport must be used before the duration.

2 Complete the sentences.

1 从我家到 ________ 走路 ________。

2 从市中心到 ________ 开车 ________。

3 从伦敦到 ________ 坐飞机 ________。

Using 以后/……的时候

1 Look at the sentences.

Adverbial clause		Main sentence/Action 2
Action 1	以后	
离开高速公路	以后，	再开大约十分钟。
After leaving the motorway, drive on for about ten minutes.		
回北京	以后，	我们可以看京剧。
After going back to Beijing, we can watch Beijing opera.		

Adverbial clause		Main sentence/Action 2
Action 1	的时候	
我到教室	的时候，	老师已经在上课了。
When I got to the classroom, the teacher was already giving the class.		
去西安旅行	的时候，	你会穿什么衣服？
What will you wear when you go travelling to Xi'an?		

Now check the two correct explanations.

☐ 1 以后 and ……的时候 are used at the beginning of an adverbial clause, meaning "after" and "when" respectively.

☐ 2 The positions of 以后 and ……的时候 in Chinese sentences are different from where "after" and "when" are placed in English sentences.

☐ 3 以后 and ……的时候 can not be used to express the same concept of time.

2 Write the sentences in Chinese.

1 I called my mother after I arrived in Beijing.

2 She was sleeping when I left home.

3 I do my homework after I get back home every day.

Turn to page 162 for grammar reference.

LESSON | 3

Communication activity

1 Your class are going on a weekend trip together. As a class, discuss and agree on a destination.

2 Work in groups of four. Plan the trip, including means of transport, the best route to get there, and things to see and do on the trip.

3 Present your plan to the class.

4 Work with the whole class. Decide on the best plan.

Turn to pages 148 and 154 for more speaking practice.

Cultural corner

The art of paper-cutting

Paper-cuttings, common souvenirs often found in markets and temple fairs around China, are a traditional form of folk art. Paper was a precious commodity in very ancient times, and none but the very wealthiest could have afforded to use it for artwork. But as paper became more widely available, paper-cutting became a popular art form, allowing everyone, from high-born courtiers to lowly artisans, to express their creativity with just a pair of scissors and a few sheets of paper.

In parts of rural China, paper-cutting is a traditional activity for women, and skill at paper-cutting used to be considered a great advantage in a prospective bride.

Paper-cuts were traditionally used for religious rites, ornamentation and portraits. Nowadays, they are most commonly used as decorations on walls, windows, mirrors and lanterns. They also make good gifts for friends, and are a popular choice as souvenirs.

Character writing

These are two common radicals in Chinese. Do you know any other characters with the same radicals?

Radical	Meaning	Examples
礻	spirit	礼、福
纟	silk	纸、绿

1 Look at the characters and identify the radicals.

祝　给　级　视

2 Match the words with the meanings.

1 终于　　a TV
2 祝　　b at last
3 电视　　c approximately
4 大约　　d wish

3 Trace the characters in the boxes.

视

祝

约

终

Review and practice

1 Match the words with the meanings.

1 堵车　　a arrive
2 拐　　b stuck/caught in traffic
3 进入　　c leave
4 到达　　d enter
5 离开　　e turn

2 Write four sentences about your daily activities using 以后 and ……的时候.

3 Work in pairs. Ask and answer questions about how far away the following places are from your home, and how to get to them.

1 学校　　2 北京
3 地铁站　　4 香港
5 飞机场　　6 伦敦

4 Write two sentences to describe each picture, including the means of transport.

a

b

Vocabulary extension

Look at Mark's train ticket and complete the text message.

chē
车 carriage of a train
èrděngzuò
二等座 second-class seat
dàngrì
当日 on the date stated

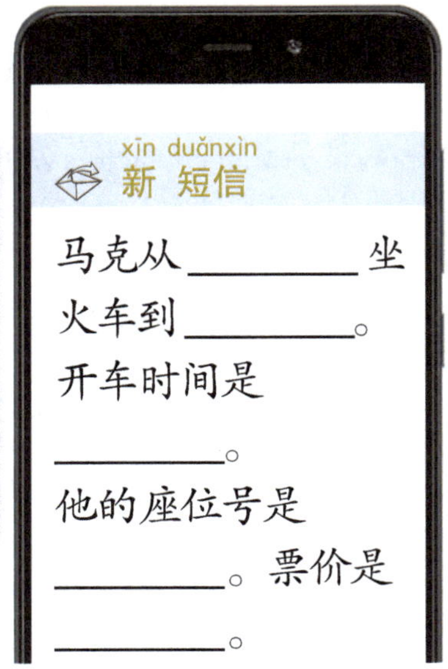

Vocabulary review

Fill in the blanks.

比较	bǐjiào	*adv.*	comparatively
不过	búguò	*conj.*	however, but
宾馆	bīnguǎn	*n.*	________
博物馆	bówùguǎn	*n.*	museum
____	bú kèqi		you're welcome
车费	chēfèi	*n.*	(passenger) fare
到达	dàodá	*v.*	arrive
大约	dàyuē	*adv.*	________
堵车	dǔchē	*v.*	________
高速公路	gāosù gōnglù	*n.*	motorway, freeway
____	gōngjiāo		public transport
____	gōnglǐ	*n.*	kilometre
古	gǔ	*adj.*	________
拐	guǎi	*v.*	turn
换乘	huàn chéng		transfer
进入	jìnrù	*v.*	enter
____	kāi	*v.*	drive (a vehicle)
开玩笑	kāi wánxiào		________
快	kuài	*adj.*	fast
离开	líkāi	*v.*	________
路	lù	*n.*	bus route
____	màn	*adj.*	slow

____	nín	*pron.*	you (respectful form)
墙	qiáng	*n.*	wall
容易	róngyì	*adj.*	________
____	wàimiàn	*n.*	outside
向	xiàng	*prep.*	to, towards
像	xiàng	*v.*	________
右	yòu	*n.*	the right side
____	yuán	*n.*	yuan, Chinese currency unit
再见	zàijiàn	*v.*	________
咱们	zánmen	*pron.*	we, us
____	zhǎo	*v.*	look for
终于	zhōngyú	*adv.*	________
祝	zhù	*v.*	wish
____	zǒulù	*v.*	walk
线	xiàn	*n.*	line
车	chē	*n.*	carriage of a train
当日	dàngrì	*n.*	on the date stated
上/下车	shàng/xià chē	*v.*	get on/off a vehicle
二等座	èrděngzuò	*n.*	second-class seat

Review 1

Vocabulary

1 Match the verbs with the nouns to make phrases.

1 交	a 故事
2 准备	b 报纸
3 读	c 毛衣
4 看	d 考试
5 戴	e 作业
6 穿	f 手套

2 Make words using the characters in the box.

响　和　降　云　报　别　温　气

1 气 ______	2 空 ______
3 差 ______	4 下 ______
5 暖 ______	6 多 ______
7 影 ______	8 预 ______

Now make sentences using the words given.

9 空气/影响

10 预报/下降

3 Complete the sentences with the words in the box.

参加　拜年　喝　庆祝　介绍　贴

1 你能给我们 ______ 一下吗？

2 过年的时候很多人家的门口都会 ______ 春联。

3 你想 ______ 什么？果汁还是茶？

4 大年初一我去朋友家 ______。

5 很多人 ______ 了学校的除夕派对。

6 你想怎样 ______ 生日？

4 Put the words in the correct categories.

a 走路	b 下雪	c 气温
d 拜年	e 开车	f 红灯笼
g 堵车	h 晴	i 转乘
j 红包	k 春联	l 阴

天气	春节	交通

Now write five sentences about what Chinese people do during the Spring Festival.

Grammar

1 Match the parts to complete the sentences.

1 星期一的考试，

2 公园离我家不远，

3 我一回家，

4 我们先吃饭，

5 你去看电影的时候，

6 从这里到市中心，

a 王玉正在学校上课。

b 坐公共汽车要半个小时。

c 我准备好了。

d 走路只要十分钟。

e 就给她打电话。

f 然后去看电影。

2 Complete the sentences using 就 or 才.

1 电影开始以后马克 ____ 来。

2 早上六点半王玉 ____ 起床了。

3 他今天很累，晚上八点 ____ 上床睡觉了。

4 老师已经开始上课了他 ____ 来。

3 Complete the sentences using 要 or 会.

1 今天晚上我不能跟你们一起看电影了，我 ____ 复习准备考试。

2 下个月气温 ____ 下降很多。

3 下雨了，他今天不 ____ 来了。

4 Make sentences using 又……又…… and the words given.

1 便宜/漂亮

2 读故事/看报纸

3 唱歌/玩游戏

5 Write a sentence to describe each picture, using 得 to indicate the result or degree.

a

b

6 Write three sentences about what you did yesterday, using 得 to indicate the result or degree.

7 Write three sentences about things you often do at the same time, using 一边……一边…….

8 Complete the sentences using 以后 and …… 的时候.

1 起床 ________，我洗脸刷牙。

2 马克来我家 _______，我正在贴春联。

3 放学 _______，他们去打篮球。

4 暑假 ______，我们要去上海旅行。

9 Write four sentences to describe your city or town, using A 比/没有 B + adjective and A 和 B + 差不多/一样.

Integrated skills

37

1 Listen and choose the correct answers to the questions.

1 他住在伦敦的时候每天上课前都做什么？

a 打网球　　b 跑步

2 他在这里每天上课前都去跑步吗？

a 去　　b 不去

3 哪里的天气比较冷？

a 成都　　b 首尔

4 去成都需要带很多衣服吗？

a 需要　　b 不需要

5 人们怎样庆祝新年？

a 贴春联　　b 挂红灯笼

6 春联贴在哪里？

a 门口　　b 卧室

7 怎么去邮局？

a 往前走三十米，再向左拐。

b 往前走三十米，再向右拐。

38

2 Listen and choose the most appropriate responses.

1 a 对不起，我要复习准备明天的考试。

b 我们可以下次一起跑步。

2 a 下雪？没问题，我可以多穿一些衣服。

b 太好了！那我可以穿我最喜欢的T恤和短裤了！

3 a 新年好！谢谢阿姨。

b 太好了。

4 a 我给你们介绍一下。

b 我带你们参观一下我家。

5 a 火车站离市中心不远，坐出租车十分钟就到了。

b 火车站离这里很近，走路就可以到。

6 a 兵马俑很远，你们可以坐旅游客车去。

b 兵马俑在西安市东边三十公里。

3 **Complete the passage using the words in the box.**

方便	冷	暖和	穿
天气	景点	历史	戴

西安在中国的西北部。这里四个季节的 ______ 都不一样：春天 ______，夏天很热，秋天凉爽，冬天很 ______。夏天可以 ______ 裙子、T恤和短裤；冬天要 ______ 毛衣和大衣，______ 围巾和手套。

西安有几千年的 ______，有很多有名的 ______。最有名的是秦始皇兵马俑博物馆。西安的交通很 ______，你可以坐火车或者飞机去西安。

Now read again and check the true statements.

☐ 1 西安四个季节的天气都差不多。

☐ 2 冬天去西安不能穿短裤。

☐ 3 西安的景点不太有名。

☐ 4 你只能坐飞机去西安。

4 **Write about your travel plans for the winter holidays, including time, place, weather, what to wear, transport and highlights of the place. Make comparisons between the places you have considered and state reasons for your choice. Use 先……然后……, A 比 B + adjective, 又……又…….**

Enjoy Chinese

打

The character 打 is formed by the radical 扌 and the signific 丁. In ancient Chinese, the radical 扌 was 手 and the signific 丁 was 个. In modern Chinese, 打 is a common verb and can form a wide range of verb phrases indicating different activities. Here are some examples.

打网球	play tennis
打电话	make a phone call
打车	take a taxi

Now match the phrases with the meanings.

1 打水	a do a temporary job
2 打工	b play cards
3 打牌	c draw water

UNIT 5

Qǐngwèn nín yùdìng fángjiān le ma
请问 您预订房间了吗？

Do you have a reservation?

LESSON 1

Vocabulary and listening

39 **1 Check the furniture that you can find in the picture.**

- ☐ yīguì 衣柜
- ☐ shāfā 沙发
- ☐ chuáng 床
- ☐ shūguì 书柜
- ☐ zhuōzi 桌子
- ☐ yǐzi 椅子

Now listen and say the words.

40 **2 Match the phrases with the meanings.**

1 yùdìng fángjiān 预订 房间	a fill in a registration card
2 bànlǐ rùzhù 办理 入住	b take a room card
3 tián dēngjì kǎ 填 登记 卡	c reserve a room
4 ná fángkǎ 拿 房卡	d check in

Now listen and say the phrases.

41 **3 Mark, Amanda and Yeong-min are checking in at their hotel in Xi'an. Listen to the conversation and answer the questions.**

1 马克有没有预订房间？
2 服务员为什么要问马克的手机号码？
3 阿曼达为什么打电话给服务员？

服务员：您好！欢迎光临古城宾馆。
马克：你好。我们想办理入住。
服务员：请问您预订房间了吗？
马克：预订了。我叫Mark Johnson。
服务员：请给我看一下你们的护照。
阿曼达和永民：给你。
服务员：你们订了一个标准间和一个单人间，一共四天，对吗？
马克：对。
服务员：请填一下入住登记卡。
马克：好的。…… 填完了，给你。
服务员：谢谢。…… 请问您的手机号码是16628958963吗？
马克：不是，我的手机号是16628958763。这是7，不是9。
服务员：好的，你们的房间号是826和832。这是房卡。

阿曼达：请问房间里可以上网吗？
服务员：可以。

[在房间里]
服务员：喂，您好！请问有什么可以帮助您的吗？
阿曼达：你好！我想上网，但是不知道wi-fi密码。
服务员：密码就在房卡的背面。
阿曼达：能不能再给我一床被子，这里很冷。
服务员：您房间的洗手间对面有一个衣柜，衣柜的最上面有一床被子，您可以拿出来用。
阿曼达：谢谢你，再见。

New words

fúwùyuán 服务员	attendant, waiter, waitress	dēngjì 登记	register
huānyíng 欢迎	welcome	lǐ 里	inside
guānglín 光临	be present	shàngwǎng 上网	go online
bànlǐ 办理	handle	bāngzhù 帮助	help
rùzhù 入住	check in	mìmǎ 密码	password
yùdìng 预订	reserve	bèimiàn 背面	back
hùzhào 护照	passport	bèizi 被子	quilt
biāozhǔn 标准	standard	yīguì 衣柜	wardrobe
dānrén 单人	single person	ná 拿	take, get
yígòng 一共	altogether	chū 出	go/come out
tián 填	fill in		

41

4 **Listen again and check the correct words or phrases to complete the sentences.**

1 服务员要看他们的 ________。
☐ a 护照 ☐ b 登记卡

2 被子在 ________。
☐ a 衣柜的上面 ☐ b 桌子的下面

5 **Work in pairs. Look at the booking information and act out a conversation between a receptionist at the hotel and a tourist checking into the hotel.**

华伟酒店

姓名	马大伟	天数	两天
房间	一个单人间	房价	¥500/天

Pronunciation and speaking

Tone sandhi: 3rd + 3rd tones

42

1 Look at the tone mark for the first character of each word. How does the tone change?

1	你好	ní hǎo
2	洗手间	xíshǒujiān
3	给你	géi nǐ
4	可以	kéyǐ

Now listen and repeat.

43

2 Listen and check the tones you hear.

1	我想	☐ wó xiǎng	☐ wǒ xiǎng
2	很冷	☐ hén lěng	☐ hěn lěng
3	景点	☐ jíngdiǎn	☐ jǐngdiǎn
4	很好	☐ hén hǎo	☐ hěn hǎo

Now listen again and repeat.

44

3 Say the sentences aloud.

Kéyǐ géi wǒ kàn yíxià nín de hùzhào ma
1 可以 给 我 看 一下 您 的 护照 吗？

Wó xiǎng qù hěn duō hǎowánr de jíngdiǎn
2 我 想 去 很 多 好玩儿 的 景点。

Wǒ kéyǐ géi nǐ zhǎo yíxià
3 我 可以 给 你 找 一下。

Now listen and repeat.

45

4 Listen and say the words.

1	yīguì 衣柜	zhuōzi 桌子	yǐzi 椅子	xǐshǒujiān 洗手间
2	hùzhào 护照	bèizi 被子	fángkǎ 房卡	dēngjì kǎ 登记 卡
3	duìmiàn 对面	bèimiàn 背面	pángbiān 旁边	shàngmiàn 上面

5 Write down what things would be in your dream hotel room and their locations.

6 Work in pairs.

A: Describe your hotel room to B using the information in Activity 5.

B: Draw a picture of A's room.

Now change roles.

7 Check each other's pictures to see if they match the description in Activity 5.

CHINESE TO GO

46

Accommodation expressions

Yǒu kōngfáng ma 有 空房 吗？	Do you have any vacancies?
Hán zǎocān ma 含 早餐 吗？	Is breakfast included?
Wǒ xiǎng dìng fáng 我 想 订 房。	I'd like to book a room.
Wǒ yào tuì fáng 我 要 退 房。	I'd like to check out.
Kěyǐ shuākǎ ma 可以 刷卡 吗？	Can I pay by credit/debit card?

LESSON 2

Reading and writing

1 Match the words with the things in the picture.

- [ ] a máojīn 毛巾
- [ ] b féizào 肥皂
- [ ] c yáshuā 牙刷
- [ ] d tìxūdāo 剃须刀
- [ ] e yágāo 牙膏
- [ ] f shūzi 梳子

Now check the things you use every day.

47

2 Read the website comments from Amanda and another hotel guest about the hotel in Xi'an, and answer the questions.

1 阿曼达觉得古城宾馆怎么样?

2 王伟觉得这个宾馆怎么样?

New words

jiē 街	street	
chuángdān 床单	bed sheet	
máojīn 毛巾	towel	
gānjìng 干净	clean	
rìyòngpǐn 日用品	daily necessity	
yágāo 牙膏	toothpaste	
yáshuā 牙刷	toothbrush	
féizào 肥皂	soap	
shūzi 梳子	comb	
miǎnfèi 免费	free of charge	
xǐyī 洗衣	wash clothes	
xǐ 洗	wash	
zhènghǎo 正好	just right	
shūfu 舒服	comfortable	
lìngwài 另外	in addition, besides	
cháng 长	length, long	
kuān 宽	width, wide	
gòu 够	be enough	
gèzi 个子	height	

爱旅游　爱生活　请选择　搜索

旅游宝典　景区住宿　景区美图　旅游攻略　旅游投诉

陕西>西安

用户评级
208人推荐
45人不推荐

古城宾馆
星级：★★★
地区：西安市中心
地址：西安市西大街18号

推荐　阿曼达

这个宾馆在市中心，交通很方便。这里的房间很不错，床单和毛巾都很干净。房间里的日用品，比如牙膏、牙刷、肥皂和梳子等，都是免费的。宾馆的洗衣服务又快又好，我下午拿大衣去洗，晚上就洗好了。有人觉得房间太小了，但是我觉得房间的大小正好，很舒服。另外，房间里可以上网，很方便。

不推荐　王伟

宾馆的交通很方便，服务也很好，但是房间太小了。我住的房间长3米，宽2.5米，比其他宾馆的房间小多了。房间里的床也不够大，单人床长1.8米，宽1.2米，个子高的人就不够用了。

3 **Check the true statements.**

☐ 1 房间里的毛巾和床单不太干净。
☐ 2 房间里的日用品都是免费的。
☐ 3 阿曼达觉得房间太小了。
☐ 4 王伟觉得房间和床的大小正好。

4 **Read again and list the positive and negative things Amanda and Wang Wei said about the hotel.**

5 **Write some comments about a hotel you know, including transportation, room facilities and service. Describe both the good and bad points. Use the descriptions in Activity 2 to help you.**

Language in use

Indicating possession, existence or location with 有

1 **Look at the sentences.**

Subject	Verb	Noun phrase
我	有	中文报纸。
她	有	一件大衣。
一天	有	二十四小时。

Now check the two correct explanations.

☐ 1 有 is used to say that someone possesses something.
☐ 2 The subject of a possessive sentence with 有 must be a person.
☐ 3 有 means "have", "own" or "possess".

2 **Look at the sentences.**

Locative phrase		Verb	Noun phrase
Attribute	Location		
洗手间的	对面	有	一个衣柜。
衣柜的	最上面	有	一床被子。
学校	附近	没有	超市。

Now check the two correct explanations.

☐ 1 有 is used to indicate the existence or location of a place or something in relation to another.
☐ 2 The locative phrase often contains a place or object that is smaller in size than what is contained in the noun phrase.
☐ 3 有 means "exist" or "there is/are".

3 **Answer the questions using 有.**

1 学校附近有什么？
2 教室里有什么？
3 你有哥哥或者姐姐吗？你家有几个人？

Indicating adequacy with 够/不够

1 Look at the sentences.

Attribute	Subject	Verb	Complement
这个	房子	够	大。
我的	时间	不够	用。
	饭菜	不够	吃。

Now check the two correct explanations.

☐ 1 够 and 不够 are used to indicate whether something is sufficient for a particular purpose.

☐ 2 The complement of the verb 够 can be an adjective or a verb.

☐ 3 够 and 不够 can be put after the complement to indicate adequacy.

2 Write the sentences in Chinese.

1 This dress is not long enough.
2 There is enough time to finish the homework.
3 There are enough people to complete the work.

Complements indicating results

1 Look at the sentences.

Subject	Verb	Complement
我	填	完了。
衣服	洗	好了。
我	找	不到wi-fi密码。

Now check the two correct explanations.

☐ 1 Only an adjective can be used after a verb to indicate the result of an action.

☐ 2 After a verb, another verb or verb phrase can be used to indicate the result of an action.

☐ 3 The subject of a verb can be a person or a thing.

2 Write the sentences in Chinese.

1 I have finished doing my homework.
2 Did you see her?
3 Dinner is ready.

Questions about sizes with （有）多大/长/宽

1 Look at the sentences.

Subject	Predicate	
	Verb	Question word
房间	（有）	多大/长/宽？
单人床	（有）	多大/长/宽？

Subject	Verb	Measurement	Size	Measurement
房间		长	3米。	
房间		宽	2.5米。	
房子	（有）		3米	高。
单人床		长	1.8米。	
单人床		宽	1.2米。	
桌子	（有）		1米	宽。

Now check the two correct explanations.

☐ 1 多 is used before words indicating measurements to form question words about sizes.

☐ 2 The words indicating measurements can be put before or after the words for sizes.

☐ 3 A verb is required in sentences about sizes.

2 Answer the questions with your own information.

1 你多高？
2 你家的房子多大？
3 你的房间多大？

Turn to page 163 for grammar reference.

LESSON | 3

Communication activity

1 Work in groups of four. You are going on a trip to Beijing and need to find a hotel. Compare the hotels below and choose the one you like best.

华伟酒店

★★★★ ☺☺

- 房间又大又舒服：标准间长10米，宽5米
- 免费洗衣，免费日用品
- 房价比较贵，1300元/天
- 到机场坐出租车大约5分钟，到市中心坐出租车要1小时左右。

朝阳宾馆

★★★ ☺☺☺

- 房间不大不小：标准间长8米，宽4米
- 免费日用品，可以上网
- 房价不贵，500元/天
- 离朝阳公园很近，到天安门坐出租车只要30分钟。

前门宾馆

★ ☺☺

- 房间比较小：标准间长4米，宽3米
- 单人床不够大，公用洗手间，免费旅游指南
- 房价很便宜，300元/天，但是服务不太好。
- 在市中心，离天安门200米，交通很方便。

2 Make a list of the reasons for your choice.

3 Present your choice and reasons to another group.

▶ Turn to pages 149 and 155 for more speaking practice.

Cultural corner

Family inns in the countryside

Chinese people are well known for their hospitality. Hosts are expected to serve their guests with the best they have to make them feel at home. This is generally true in the countryside, where farmers or villagers provide free shelter and food even to strangers.

Due to the hustle and bustle of city life, the countryside is becoming a popular holiday destination for China's urban residents. Family inns in the countryside have their origins in traditional hospitality. They are run by local villagers who had opened up their own houses to accommodate travellers.

At family inns, guests are served home-made meals prepared by their hosts using local ingredients. They participate in farm work, experience the quiet and relaxing pace of life in the country, and enjoy the beautiful country scenery. Family inns are becoming more and more popular because of their modest cost, the hospitality of local people, and the simple, relaxing environment.

Character writing

These are two common radicals in Chinese. Do you know any other characters with the same radicals?

Radical	Meaning	Examples
方	square, side	旅、旁
八	eight	分、兵

1 Look at the characters and identify the radicals.

只　房　公　旋

2 Match the words with the meanings.

1 一共	a convenient
2 房间	b kilometre
3 方便	c altogether
4 公里	d room

3 Trace the characters in the boxes.

方

房

公

共

Review and practice

1 Put the sentences in the correct order.

a 请您填一下入住登记卡。

b 再见！

c 可以给我看一下您的护照吗？

d 您的房间号是826。

e 欢迎光临！

f 您需要什么帮助？

g 希望您住得开心。

h 请问您预订房间了吗？

Now work in pairs. Act out the conversation between a hotel receptionist and a hotel guest.

2 Write three sentences about the positions of three objects you can see in the picture, using 有.

3 Answer the questions, using 够.

1 你每天睡几个小时？你觉得睡觉的时间够吗？

2 今天的天气怎么样？你穿的衣服够暖和吗？

4 Work in pairs. Ask and answer questions about the sizes of three objects you can see in the classroom.

Vocabulary extension

1 Look at the buttons on a hotel telephone.

Now match the words with the meanings.

a room service
b front desk/reception
c housekeeping
d operator

2 Work in pairs. Talk about your most recent stay at a hotel. Try to use the words from Activity 1.

Vocabulary review

Fill in the blanks.

办理	bànlǐ	*v.*	handle
______	bāngzhù	*v.*	help
背面	bèimiàn	*n.*	back
被子	bèizi	*n.*	______
标准	biāozhǔn	*n./adj.*	standard
______	cháng	*n./adj.*	length, long
______	chū	*v.*	go/come out
床单	chuángdān	*n.*	______
单人	dānrén	*n.*	single person
登记	dēngjì	*v.*	______
肥皂	féizào	*n.*	______
服务员	fúwùyuán	*n.*	attendant, waiter, waitress
干净	gānjìng	*adj.*	clean
______	gèzi	*n.*	height
够	gòu	*v.*	______
光临	guānglín	*v.*	be present
护照	hùzhào	*n.*	______
______	huānyíng	*v.*	welcome
街	jiē	*n.*	street
宽	kuān	*n./adj.*	______
______	lǐ	*n.*	inside
另外	lìngwài	*conj.*	in addition, besides
毛巾	máojīn	*n.*	towel
密码	mìmǎ	*n.*	password

免费	miǎnfèi	*v.*	______
拿	ná	*v.*	______
日用品	rìyòngpǐn	*n.*	______
______	rùzhù	*v.*	check in
上网	shàngwǎng	*v.*	go online
舒服	shūfu	*adj.*	comfortable
梳子	shūzi	*n.*	______
填	tián	*v.*	fill in
洗	xǐ	*v.*	wash
______	xǐyī	*v.*	wash clothes
牙膏	yágāo	*n.*	toothpaste
牙刷	yáshuā	*n.*	toothbrush
衣柜	yīguì	*n.*	wardrobe
______	yígòng	*adv.*	altogether
预订	yùdìng	*v.*	______
正好	zhènghǎo	*adj.*	just right
客房部	kèfáng bù	*n.*	housekeeping
前台	qiántái	*n.*	front desk/ reception
沙发	shāfā	*n.*	sofa
送餐服务	sòngcān fúwù	*n.*	room service
剃须刀	tìxūdāo	*n.*	razor
椅子	yǐzi	*n.*	chair
总机	zǒngjī	*n.*	operator

UNIT 6

Jìnzhǐ pāizhào
禁止拍照！
No photography!

LESSON | 1

Vocabulary and listening

48

1 Match the signs with the meanings.

a

b

c

d

1 jìnzhǐ pāizhào 禁止 拍照

2 bùdé rù nèi 不得 入内

3 ānjìng 安静

4 yánjìn yǐnshí 严禁 饮食

Now listen and say the phrases.

49

2 Mark, Amanda and Yeong-min go to see the Terracotta Warriors. Listen to the conversation and answer the questions.

1 学生票多少钱一张？
2 兵马俑是谁发现的？
3 永民觉得那个兵俑像谁？
4 他们看到了什么指示牌？

售票员：您好。
马克：你好。请给我三张学生票。
售票员：可以给我看看学生证吗？
马克：给你。
售票员：谢谢。这是三张票，一共180元。你们的导游会在入口处等你们。

［在博物馆里］
永民：请问兵马俑是怎么被发现的？
导游：1974年，当地的农民在打井的时候发现了兵马俑。这个兵俑高1.83米，和真人差不多高。
阿曼达：当时的中国人真的有1.83米高吗？现在大部分人都没有那么高。
导游：它可能比当时的人高一点儿。
永民：这个兵俑看起来很像我们的汉

语老师——丁老师，你们觉得呢？

阿曼达：是啊，他看起来很像我们没交作业时的丁老师，哈哈……

导游：嘘…… 请安静，这里不能大声说话。

马克：我们应该拍张照片送给丁老师。

永民：等一下，那个指示牌上写着“禁止拍照”。

马克：对不起，我没有看到。

阿曼达：我想过去看看那个兵马俑有多高。

马克：不要过去，这个指示牌上写着“不得入内”。

阿曼达：啊？什么都不可以……

New words

shòupiàoyuán 售票员	ticket seller	nóngmín 农民	farmer
zhāng 张	(uesd for paper, paintings, etc)	jǐng 井	well
piào 票	ticket	dāngshí 当时	that time
zhèng 证	certificate	Hànyǔ 汉语	Chinese (language)
dǎoyóu 导游	tour guide	xū 嘘	shh
rùkǒu chù 入口处	entrance	ānjìng 安静	quiet
děng 等	wait for	shēng 声	voice
bèi 被	(used in the passive voice to introduce the doer of the action or the action if the doer is not mentioned)	sòng 送	give (as a gift)
		zhǐshìpái 指示牌	sign, notice-board
		zhe 着	(used to indicate the continuation of an action or a state)
fāxiàn 发现	discover	jìnzhǐ 禁止	forbid
dāngdì 当地	local		

49

3 **Listen again and check the true statements.**

☐ 1 他们的导游会在售票处等他们。

☐ 2 那个兵俑和当时的中国人一样高。

☐ 3 博物馆里不能拍照。

4 **Work in pairs. Look at the signs and guess the meanings.**

a

b

5 **Make some signs showing rules for visitors to your home. Don't use any words on your signs.**

Now work in pairs. Guess the meanings of your partner's signs.

Pronunciation and speaking

Difference between "ü" and "üe"

50 **1** **Check the correct finals for the underlined characters.**

1 学生 ☐ ü ☐ üe
2 汉语 ☐ ü ☐ üe
3 觉得 ☐ ü ☐ üe
4 大约 ☐ ü ☐ üe
5 京剧 ☐ ü ☐ üe
6 音乐 ☐ ü ☐ üe

Now listen and repeat.

51 **2** **Read the sentences aloud.**

1 Míngtiān huì xià dà yǔ
明天会下大雨。

2 Wǒ juéde jīngjù hěn hǎotīng
我觉得京剧很好听。

3 Jīnnián Liùyuè wǒ yào qù Guìlín lǚyóu
今年六月我要去桂林旅游。

4 Wáng Yù hé Mǎkè yào qù tīng yīnyuèhuì
王玉和马克要去听音乐会。

5 Xīn tóngxué de jiā zǒulù dàyuē shí fēnzhōng
新同学的家走路大约十分钟。

Now listen and repeat.

52 **3** **Listen and say the words.**

1	zhǐshìpái 指示牌	jìnzhǐ 禁止	bùdé 不得	ānjìng 安静
2	shòupiàoyuán 售票员	dǎoyóu 导游	nóngmín 农民	rùkǒu chù 入口处
3	kàn qǐlái 看起来	dāngshí 当时	fāxiàn 发现	dǎ jǐng 打井

4 **Write down information about a famous historical site that you are familiar with, including its location, size, how old it is, what it is for and why it is significant.**

Now work in pairs. Ask and answer questions about each other's sites. Try to work out what your partner's site is.

CHINESE TO GO

53 Expressions for visiting tourist attractions

Jǐ diǎn kāimén 几点开门？	What time do you open?
Ménpiào duōshao qián yì zhāng 门票多少钱一张？	How much is one ticket?
Chūkǒu zài nǎr 出口在哪儿？	Where is the exit?
Jiǎnjiè yǒu Yīngwén de ma 简介有英文的吗？	Do you have an English brochure?

LESSON 2

Reading and writing

1 Work in pairs. Discuss what you know about these words.

1 Hàncháo 汉朝　2 Tángrén 唐人　3 Hànzì 汉字

54

2 Read Mark's online post about his trip to the Shaanxi History Museum and answer the questions.

1 什么是"汉语"？它是怎样得名的?
2 为什么中国城被称为"唐人街"？

New words

wàn	万	ten thousand	wénzì	文字	writing, script
wénwù	文物	cultural relic	qiángshèng	强盛	powerful and prosperous
liǎojiě	了解	understand	cháodài	朝代	dynasty
shù	数	number, figure	zhī yī	之一	one of
mínzú	民族	ethnic group	hǎiwài	海外	overseas
Hànzú	汉族	Han ethnic group	chēng	称	call, weigh
démíng	得名	get one's name	suǒyǐ	所以	therefore
yú	于	at, in			

博客首页　登录　注册　发博文　博文　搜索

首页 | 博文 | 图片 | 关于我

马克的资料

进入我的空间

加好友　发纸条
写留言　加关注

我的博文

陕西历史博物馆

来西安的第三天，我们参观了陕西历史博物馆。博物馆里大约有 171 万件文物，是了解中国历史的好地方。

博物馆里有很多汉朝（公元前 206 年—公元 220 年）的文物。中国人数最多的民族——汉族，就得名于汉朝。汉族人说的话叫汉语，他们用的文字叫汉字。当然现在大部分中国人都会说汉语，写汉字。

这是唐朝（公元 618年—907 年）的文物，叫唐三彩。唐朝是中国历史上最强盛的朝代之一。最早去海外的中国人称他们自己为"唐人"，所以中国城也叫"唐人街"。

3 Read again and check the true statements.

- ☐ 1 汉族人说的话叫汉语。
- ☐ 2 汉族是中国人数最少的民族。
- ☐ 3 唐三彩是汉朝的文物。
- ☐ 4 唐人街是中国人住的地方。

4 Complete the timeline using the information in Mark's online post.

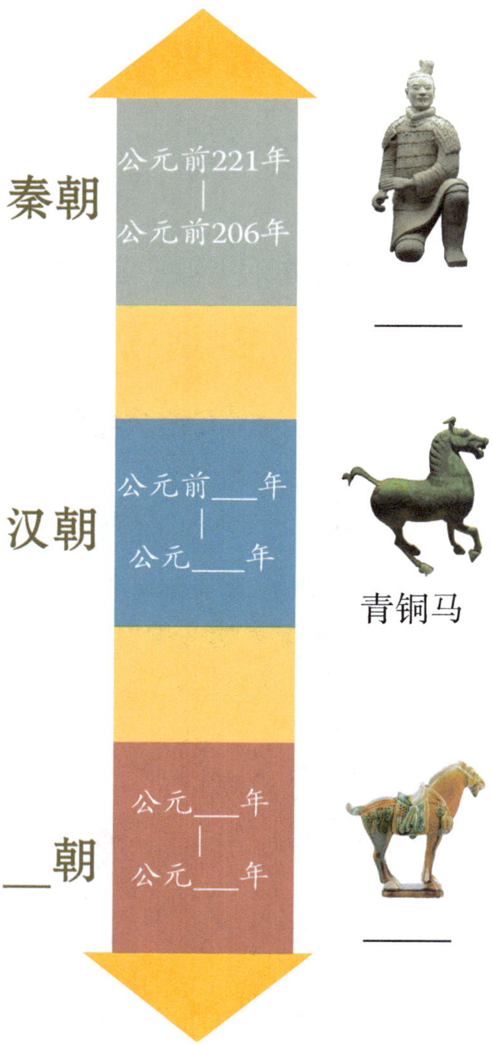

5 Write about a historical period that you are familiar with, including its timeframe, notable people and what it is famous for.

Language in use

Indicating passive voice using 被

1 Look at the sentences.

Subject	Adverb	Verb	Object	Complement
当地的农民		发现了	兵马俑。	
最早去海外的中国人		称	自己	为“唐人”。
马克		拿走了	永民的护照。	
弟弟	没	吃	你的饺子。	

Subject	Adverb	Adverbial		Verb	Complement
		被	Doer		
兵马俑		被	当地的农民	发现	了。
最早去海外的中国人		被	（他们自己）	称	为“唐人”。
永民的护照		被	（马克）	拿	走了。
你的饺子	没	被	（弟弟）	吃	掉。

Now check the two correct explanations.

- ☐ 1 被 is used to make a passive sentence, emphasising the subject being acted upon.
- ☐ 2 被 can be placed after the verb in the passive voice.
- ☐ 3 The doer of the action can be omitted in the passive voice.

2 Rewrite the sentences using 被.

1. 她吃了我的晚饭。
2. 他拿走了我的书。
3. 人们称她为“马大姐”。
4. 人们称海外中国人住的地方为“唐人街”。

Indicating a continuing action or state with 着

1 Look at the sentences.

Subject	Verb	Auxiliary word	Complement
这个指示牌上	写	着	“禁止拍照”。
那个指示牌上	写	着	“不得入内”。
桌子上	放	着	两张电影票。
王玉家门口	贴	着	春联。
她	穿	着	一件大衣。

Now check the two correct explanations.

- ☐ 1 着 is used after a verb to indicate the continuation of an action or a state.
- ☐ 2 着 is used after a verb only to indicate an ongoing action in the present.
- ☐ 3 着 is used before the complement of the verb.

2 Write the sentences in Chinese using 着.

1 A book is on the table.
2 I'm wearing a green T-shirt.
3 Two red lanterns are hanging on the gate.

是……的 constructions

1 Look at the sentences.

Subject	是	Time/Place/Manner	Predicate	的
兵马俑	是	什么时候	发现	的？
兵马俑	是	1974 年	发现	的。
这些照片	是	在桂林	拍	的。
你	（是）	怎么	去	的？
我	（是）	坐火车	去	的。
我	不是	坐火车	去	的。

Now check the two correct explanations.

- ☐ 1 是……的 is used to talk about a certain aspect of a past action or event, such as when, where or how.
- ☐ 2 是 is usually placed right after the subject and cannot be omitted.
- ☐ 3 的 is put at the end of the sentence and cannot be omitted.

2 Write questions about the underlined parts of the sentences using 是……的.

1 马克去年去桂林旅行。
2 我在北京认识王玉。
3 安娜坐飞机去新加坡。

Turn to page 164 for grammar reference.

LESSON | 3

Communication activity

1 Work in groups of three. Choose a dynasty from page 74. Find out more about this dynasty and complete the table.

Dynasty	
Time period	
Notable people	
Most important city	
Why it is famous	
Museum(s) to recommend	

Now prepare a presentation about the dynasty. Find pictures to make your presentation interesting.

2 Work with two other groups who chose different dynasties. Give your presentation.

Turn to pages 149 and 155 for more speaking practice.

Cultural corner

Tang poetry

The Tang Dynasty represented a golden age for Chinese poetry. Over 48,000 poems by more than 2,200 poets survive from the period, and doubtless many more poems were written at the time. Although centuries old, many Tang poems are still widely read in China today.

Tang poets worked in the ancient style, but also developed new forms requiring great skill. The poems of the Tang Dynasty have a wide range of subjects, from social concerns to patriotic fervour, encompassing realism, romanticism, natural beauty and personal feelings.

The Tang era saw the birth of some of China's most famous poets, including Li Bai, Du Fu, Wang Wei and Bai Juyi. Poems by these poets and others became the prototypes for centuries of Chinese poetry that followed, and many people in China today can still recite one or two from memory.

Jìng yè sī
静夜思
李白

In the Still of the Night
by Li Bai

Chuáng qián míngyuè guāng
床前明月光，

Bright moonlight at
the foot of my bed –

Yí shì dì shàng shuāng
疑是地上霜。

Could there have
been a frost already?

Jǔtóu wàng míngyuè
举头望明月，

Lifting my head, I look
to the bright moon,

Dītóu sī gùxiāng
低头思故乡。

Sinking back again, I
think of home.

Character writing

These are two common radicals in Chinese. Do you know any other characters with the same radicals?

Radical	Meaning	Examples
彡	bristle	影、彩
厂	house	厅、厨

1 Look at the characters and identify the radicals.

雁　衫　参　厕

2 Match the words with the meanings.

1 参观　　a history
2 历史　　b living room
3 电影　　c visit
4 客厅　　d film

3 Trace the characters in the boxes.

参 彩 历 厅

Review and practice

1 Circle the odd word out in each line.

1	民族	农民	导游	售票员
2	文字	朝代	强盛	海外
3	参观	发现	禁止	安静
4	送	所以	了解	得名

2 Write the sentences in Chinese.

1 My ticket was taken by him.
2 Xi'an is known as an ancient city.
3 This story book has been borrowed by Mark.

3 Write two sentences about what you did yesterday.

Now write questions about your sentences using 是……的.

4 Work in pairs. Talk about what you see in the classroom, using 着.

5 Match the meanings with the signs.

1 售票处/在这里买票　2 禁止使用手机
3 安全出口/从这里离开　4 严禁饮食

a

b

c

d

Vocabulary extension

Match the words with the signs.

1 失物 招领 (shīwù zhāolǐng)　　2 禁止 饮酒 (jìnzhǐ yǐnjiǔ)

3 禁止 宠物 入内 (jìnzhǐ chǒngwù rù nèi)　　4 禁止 吸烟 (jìnzhǐ xīyān)

a

b

c

d

Now work in pairs. Write complete sentences to explain these signs.

Vocabulary review

Fill in the blanks.

安静	ānjìng	*adj.*	quiet
被	bèi	*auxiliary word*	(used in the passive voice to introduce the doer of the action or the action if the doer is not mentioned)
朝代	cháodài	*n.*	dynasty
称	chēng	*v.*	call, weigh
当地	dāngdì	*n.*	______
______	dāngshí	*n.*	that time
导游	dǎoyóu	*n.*	______
得名	démíng	*v.*	get one's name
______	děng	*v.*	wait for
发现	fāxiàn	*v.*	______
海外	hǎiwài	*n.*	overseas
______	Hànyǔ	*n.*	Chinese (language)
汉族	Hànzú	*n.*	Han ethnic group
禁止	jìnzhǐ	*v.*	______
井	jǐng	*n.*	well
了解	liǎojiě	*v.*	______
民族	mínzú	*n.*	ethnic group
______	nóngmín	*n.*	farmer
强盛	qiángshèng	*adj.*	______
入口处	rùkǒu chù	*n.*	entrance
声	shēng	*n.*	voice

售票员	shòupiàoyuán	*n.*	______
张	zhāng	*measure word*	(uesd for paper, paintings, etc)
票	piào	*n.*	ticket
数	shù	*n.*	______
______	sòng	*v.*	give (as a gift)
所以	suǒyǐ	*conj.*	______
______	wàn	*num.*	ten thousand
文物	wénwù	*n.*	cultural relic
______	wénzì	*n.*	writing, script
嘘	xū	*interj.*	shh
于	yú	*prep.*	at, in
______	zhe	*auxiliary word*	(used to indicate the continuation of an action or a state)
证	zhèng	*n.*	certificate
之一	zhī yī	*n.*	______
指示牌	zhǐshìpái	*n.*	sign, notice-board
宠物	chǒngwù	*n.*	pet
失物招领	shīwù zhāolǐng		lost and found
吸烟	xīyān	*v.*	smoke (tobacco)
饮酒	yǐnjiǔ	*v.*	drink alcohol
饮食	yǐnshí	*n./v.*	food and drink, eat and drink

UNIT 7

Sìchuān cài yòu má yòu là
四川菜又麻又辣!
Sichuan food is really spicy!

LESSON | 1

Vocabulary and listening

55 **1** **Work in pairs. Guess the flavour of each dish using the words in the box.**

má 麻	suān 酸	xián 咸
là 辣	tián 甜	xiāng 香

Tángcùyú
a 糖醋鱼

Gōngbǎo jīdīng
b 宫保 鸡丁

Now listen and say the words.

56 **2** **Mark, Yeong-min and Amanda are going out for lunch in Chengdu. Listen to the conversation and answer the questions.**

1 阿曼达喜欢吃什么？
2 为什么马克说他们应该吃川菜？
3 饭馆的拿手菜是什么？

［在出租车上］

马克：你们喜欢吃四川菜吗？

永民：我喜欢。四川菜又麻又辣，很好吃。

阿曼达：你是韩国人，当然喜欢吃辣的。我喜欢吃广东菜，不咸不辣，比较清淡。

马克：上海菜也很好吃，又甜又香。

阿曼达：你不是只爱吃麦当劳和肯德基吗？

马克：虽然我爱吃快餐，但是到了四川，我们就应该吃四川菜。

永民：饭馆就要到了。……麻烦你在右边停车。

［在饭馆］

服务员：请问你们几位？

永民：三位。

服务员：这边请。请问三位想喝什么？
马克：先给我来一瓶汽水。
阿曼达：我要一杯苹果汁。
永民：我要一杯水。
服务员：这是菜单。
永民：你们的拿手菜是什么？
服务员：麻婆豆腐、宫保鸡丁，还有水煮鱼。
永民：就要这三个菜吧。
服务员：还要其他菜吗？
阿曼达：炒鸡蛋吧，不辣。再要三碗米饭。麻烦你再给我们三双筷子和三个勺子。
服务员：好的。请稍等，饭菜很快就好。

New words

má 麻	(of food) a burning sensation to the taste
là 辣	spicy, hot
xián 咸	salty
qīngdàn 清淡	(of food) not oily or strongly flavoured
tián 甜	sweet
ài 爱	love, like
Màidāngláo 麦当劳	McDonald's
Kěndéjī 肯德基	KFC
máfan 麻烦	bother
tíng 停	stop
wèi 位	(used to refer to people)
píng 瓶	the quantity contained in a bottle, vase, jar or flask
qìshuǐ 汽水	soda water
bēi 杯	cup, glass
píngguǒzhī 苹果汁	apple juice
shuǐ 水	water
càidān 菜单	menu
chǎo 炒	stir-fry
jīdàn 鸡蛋	(chicken's) egg
wǎn 碗	bowl
mǐfàn 米饭	rice
kuàizi 筷子	chopstick
sháozi 勺子	spoon
shāo 稍	a little, slightly

56

3 Listen again and check the food they ordered.

☐ a Tángcùyú 糖醋鱼
☐ b Shuǐzhǔyú 水煮鱼
☐ c Gōngbǎo jīdīng 宫保 鸡丁
☐ d Chǎo jīdàn 炒 鸡蛋
☐ e Mápó dòufu 麻婆 豆腐
☐ f mǐfàn 米饭

4 Match the cuisines with the flavours.

1 四川菜
2 广东菜
3 上海菜

a 又甜又香
b 又麻又辣
c 比较清淡

5 Work in pairs. Ask and answer questions about the kinds of food you like, including the flavours.

Pronunciation and speaking

Difference between "en" and "eng"

57

1 Check the correct finals for the underlined characters.

1	很好吃	☐ en	☐ eng
2	肯德基	☐ en	☐ eng
3	请问	☐ en	☐ eng
4	什么	☐ en	☐ eng
5	稍等	☐ en	☐ eng
6	门口	☐ en	☐ eng

Now listen and repeat.

58

2 Say the sentences aloud.

1 Nǐ xǐhuan nǎge chéngshì
你 喜欢 哪个 城市 ？

2 Chéngdū de chuāncài hěn hǎochī
成都 的 川菜 很 好吃。

3 Qǐng wèn fùjìn yǒu Kěndéjī ma
请 问 附近 有 肯德基 吗？

4 Tā zài xuéxiào ménkǒu děng nǐ
他 在 学校 门口 等 你。

5 Qǐng shāo děng yīshēng mǎshàng jiù lái le
请 稍 等 ， 医生 马上 就 来 了。

Now listen and repeat.

59

3 Listen and say the words.

1	má 麻	là 辣	qīngdàn 清淡	tián 甜	xián 咸
2	shuǐ 水	chá 茶	qìshuǐ 汽水	guǒzhī 果汁	
3	jiǎozi 饺子	mǐfàn 米饭	jīdàn 鸡蛋	chuāncài 川菜	

4 Work in groups of three. List some typical Chinese dishes and common drinks you know. Think about their flavours.

Now use your list to create a menu.

5 Act out a conversation at a Chinese restaurant, using your menu from Activity 4.

A: You are the waiter. Ask your customers what they would like to eat and drink.
B and C: You are the customers. Ask about the flavours of the different dishes and tell the waiter what you would like to eat and drink.

60

CHINESE TO GO
Useful expressions in a restaurant

Fúwùyuán 服务员！	Waiter!/Waitress!
Mǎidān 买单。/ Jiézhàng 结账。	The bill, please.
Dǎbāo 打包。	Pack up this dish to take away.
Wǒ jiào wàimài 我叫外卖。	I'd like to order a delivery/takeaway.
Wǒ chī sù 我吃素。	I'm a vegetarian.

LESSON 2

Reading and writing

1 Work in pairs. Tell each other which of the following ingredients your family often use when cooking.

61

2 Read the recipe for Mapo tofu and answer the questions.

1 做麻婆豆腐需要哪些原料？

2 应该先炒肉还是先炒豆腐？

学做中国菜——麻婆豆腐

[原料]

豆腐300克，牛肉末100克（猪肉也可以），油少量，豆瓣酱两勺，花椒粉少量，葱、姜、蒜少量，鸡汤半碗

[时间]

10—15 分钟

[做法]

① 把豆腐切成小块儿，把葱、姜、蒜切成末。

② 把油放在锅里，加热。先放姜，然后放肉，把肉炒熟以后放在碗里。

③ 把油放在锅里，加热。先放葱、姜、蒜和豆瓣酱，炒香。然后放豆腐和肉，炒两分钟。再加入鸡汤，煮五分钟，最后加花椒粉。

麻婆豆腐

New words

yuánliào 原料	ingredient	huājiāofěn 花椒粉	fine powder of Chinese prickly ash	bǎ 把	(used to advance the object of a verb to the position before it)	guō 锅	wok, pan
kè 克	gram	cōng 葱	spring onion	qiē 切	cut	jiārè 加热	heat up
niúròumò 牛肉末	minced beef	jiāng 姜	ginger	chéng 成	change into	shú 熟	well done (meat)
zhūròu 猪肉	pork	suàn 蒜	garlic	kuài 块	piece	jiā 加	add
yóu 油	oil	tāng 汤	soup	fàng 放	put, place	zhǔ 煮	boil
shǎoliàng 少量	a small quantity of	zuòfǎ 做法	way of doing a thing			zuìhòu 最后	finally
dòubànjiàng 豆瓣酱	fermented bean sauce						

3 **Read the recipe again and put the ingredients in the order in which they are used.**

- ☐ a 鸡汤
- ☐ b 油
- ☐ c 姜末
- ☐ d 肉末
- ☐ e 葱、姜、蒜和豆瓣酱
- ☐ f 豆腐和炒熟的肉

4 **Choose a dish from the pictures on page 84 or 85. Guess the main ingredients and how to make it.**

Now write the recipe.

5 **Work in pairs. Describe how to make your dish to each other without saying the name of the dish. Guess the name of the dish that is being described.**

Language in use

Noun phrases with 的

1 **Look at the sentences.**

Subject	Verb phrase	Object/Noun phrase		
		Modifier		Head noun
永民	喜欢吃	辣	的	东西。
永民	喜欢吃	辣的。		
我	喜欢	黑色	的	裙子。
她	喜欢	白色的。		
这	不是	你	的	书。
这	不是	我的。		

Now check the two correct explanations.

- ☐ 1 的 is used after a modifier, which is usually a noun, pronoun or an adjective, to form a noun phrase.
- ☐ 2 A noun phrase with 的 should always contain a head noun.
- ☐ 3 The head noun can be left out to avoid repetition if it is known in the context.

2 **Write the sentences in Chinese.**

1. I don't like red. Do you have black ones?
2. She likes to eat sweet food.
3. I didn't bring my book. Can I borrow yours?

Giving instructions using imperatives

1 Look at the sentences.

Adverbial	Verb	Object/Complement
先	放	姜。
再	加	鸡汤。
	煮	五分钟。
给我	打	电话。

Now check the two correct explanations.

☐ 1 Imperatives are used to give instructions, make requests or raise enquiries.

☐ 2 Subjects are usually omitted from imperatives.

☐ 3 There should always be a verb in an imperative, describing the action needed.

2 Work in pairs.

A: Give two of the following instructions in Chinese.
B: Follow A's instructions.

1 Go to the front of the room and say your name.
2 Put your Chinese book under your desk.
3 Put your Chinese book on my desk.
4 Open your book and read two sentences aloud.

Now change roles.

把 sentences

1 Look at the sentences.

Subject	把	Object	Verb	Complement
	把	豆腐	切	成小块。
	把	油	放	在锅里。
她	把	被子	拿	出来了。
我	把	书	放	在桌子上。

Now check the two correct explanations.

☐ 1 把 sentences are used to indicate the effect of an action on an object.

☐ 2 The action verb is always put before the object that it acts upon.

☐ 3 A complement should always be used after the action verb.

2 Make sentences, using 把 and the given words.

1 鸡肉/切
2 葱/放
3 牛肉/切
4 中文书/放

Turn to page 165 for grammar reference.

LESSON | 3

Communication activity

Work in pairs.

A: You want to order a delivery from 辣婆婆 restaurant. Read the menu and decide which dishes you would like.

B: You are a new server at the restaurant. Familiarise yourself with the menu. Remember to ask the customer for his/her name, phone number and address when taking the order.

Là pópo
辣婆婆

Liángcài
凉菜 Cold dishes

Kǒushuǐjī ... yuán
口水鸡 *** ... 28元
steamed chicken in red chilli oil

Fūqī fèipiàn ... yuán
夫妻肺片 *** ... 25元
sliced beef and ox offal in chilli sauce

Wǔxiāng huāshēng ... yuán
五香 花生 five spice peanuts ... 8元

Sìchuān pàocài ... yuán
四川 泡菜 ** Sichuan pickles ... 8元

Rècài
热菜 Hot dishes

Shuǐzhǔ niúròu ... yuán
水煮 牛肉 *** beef in hot chilli oil ... 48元

Gōngbǎo jīdīng ... yuán
宫保 鸡丁 ** Kung Pao chicken ... 22元

Mápó dòufu ... yuán
麻婆 豆腐 *** Mapo tofu ... 12元

Chǎo jīdàn ... yuán
炒 鸡蛋 scrambled eggs ... 8元

Suānlàtāng ... yuán
酸辣汤 ** hot and sour soup ... 6元

Yángzhōu chǎofàn ... yuán
扬州 炒饭 Yangzhou fried rice ... 10元

mǐfàn ... yuán
米饭 rice ... 3元

hěn là
*** 很辣 very spicy

zhōng là
** 中 辣 moderately spicy

wēi là
* 微辣 a little spicy

Yǐnliào
饮料 Drinks

kělè ... yuán tīng
可乐 cola ... 5元/ 听

guǒzhī ... yuán bēi
果汁 fruit juice ... 8元/杯

píjiǔ ... yuán píng
啤酒 beer ... 8元/ 瓶

Now act out a phone conversation making the delivery order.

Turn to pages 150 and 156 for more speaking practice.

Cultural corner

Eating out: ordering shared dishes

Traditionally, Chinese diners choose a collection of dishes to share for the table, rather than ordering individually. Sharing food is not only a great way to try out different dishes, but is also good for balancing the flavours and nutrition of the overall meal. A hot, spicy dish can be balanced by a sweet or mild one.

Nowadays, communal serving spoons or chopsticks are often used for the shared dishes for reasons of hygiene. While Western hosts often let guests serve themselves, Chinese hosts like to encourage their guests to eat more, and may even insist on putting food on their guests' plates. "Fighting for the bill" is another act of politeness in Chinese culture that is often performed at the end of a restaurant meal. It is not considered essential to have dessert at the end of a meal, and Chinese menus usually don't have many varieties of dessert.

Character writing

These are two common radicals in Chinese. Do you know any other characters with the same radicals?

Radical	Meaning	Examples
米	rice	粘、糖
犭	animal	狗、狮

1 Look at the characters and identify the radicals.

料　粉　猪　猫

2 Match the words with the meanings.

1 原料　　　a pork
2 花椒粉　　b ingredient
3 熊猫　　　c fine powder of Chinese prickly ash
4 猪肉　　　d panda

3 Trace the characters in the boxes.

料

粉

猫

猪

Review and practice

1 Complete the mini-dialogues.

1 A: 您好! ____________?
B: 三位。
A: ____________。

2 A: 请问，____________________?
B: 我要一瓶汽水。

3 B: ____________________?
A: 我们的拿手菜是水煮鱼。

2 Number the steps for cooking spaghetti in the correct order.

☐ a 加肉酱。
☐ b 把意大利面放在开水里，煮15分钟。
☐ c 把煮熟的面拿出来，放在碗里。
☐ d 把水放在锅里，煮开。

3 Work in pairs. Write instructions for how to boil an egg, using 把 sentences when appropriate.

Vocabulary extension

Look at the words for some common drinks.

kāfēi 咖啡	coffee	hóngjiǔ 红酒	red wine
niúnǎi 牛奶	milk	báijiǔ 白酒	a clear Chinese liquor high in alcohol volume
kělè 可乐	cola	hóngchá 红茶	black tea

Now work in pairs. Ask and answer questions about your favourite drinks for breakfast, lunch and dinner.

Vocabulary review

Fill in the blanks.

____	ài	*v.*	love, like
把	bǎ	*prep.*	(used to advance the object of a verb to the position before it)
____	bēi	*n.*	cup, glass
菜单	càidān	*n.*	____
炒	chǎo	*v.*	____
成	chéng	*v.*	change into
葱	cōng	*n.*	spring onion
豆瓣酱	dòubànjiàng	*n.*	____
____	fàng	*v.*	put, place
锅	guō	*n.*	wok, pan
花椒粉	huājiāofěn	*n.*	____
____	jīdàn	*n.*	(chicken's) egg
____	jiā	*v.*	add
加热	jiārè	*v.*	____
姜	jiāng	*n.*	ginger
克	kè	*measure word*	____
肯德基	Kěndéjī	*n.*	KFC
____	kuài	*n.*	piece
筷子	kuàizi	*n.*	chopstick
辣	là	*adj.*	____
麻	má	*adj.*	____
麻烦	máfan	*v.*	____
麦当劳	Màidāngláo	*n.*	McDonald's
____	mǐfàn	*n.*	rice
牛肉末	niúròumò	*n.*	____
瓶	píng	*n.*	the quantity contained in a bottle, vase, jar or flask
____	píngguǒzhī	*n.*	apple juice
汽水	qìshuǐ	*n.*	____
切	qiē	*v.*	cut
清淡	qīngdàn	*adj.*	____
稍	shāo	*adv.*	a little, slightly
____	sháozi	*n.*	spoon
少量	shǎoliàng	*adj.*	a small quantity of
熟	shú	*adj.*	____
____	shuǐ	*n.*	water
蒜	suàn	*n.*	garlic
____	tāng	*n.*	soup
甜	tián	*adj.*	____
____	tíng	*v.*	stop
碗	wǎn	*n.*	bowl
____	wèi	*measure word*	(used to refer to people)
咸	xián	*adj.*	____
____	yóu	*n.*	oil
原料	yuánliào	*n.*	____
猪肉	zhūròu	*n.*	pork
煮	zhǔ	*v.*	____
____	zuìhòu	*n.*	finally
做法	zuòfǎ	*n.*	____
白酒	báijiǔ	*n.*	a clear Chinese liquor high in alcohol volume
红茶	hóngchá	*n.*	black tea
红酒	hóngjiǔ	*n.*	red wine
咖啡	kāfēi	*n.*	coffee
可乐	kělè	*n.*	cola
牛奶	niúnǎi	*n.*	milk
酸	suān	*adj.*	sour

UNIT 8

Kěyǐ piányi yìdiǎnr ma

可以便宜一点儿吗？

Could it be a little cheaper?

LESSON | 1

Vocabulary and listening

62

1 **Check the souvenirs you would like to buy in China.**

☐ wánjù 玩具	☐ tángzhuāng 唐装
☐ chájù 茶具	☐ máobǐ 毛笔

Now listen and say the words.

63

2 **Mark, Amanda and Yeong-min are at a market in Chengdu. Listen to the conversation and answer the questions.**

1 马克为什么要买玩具熊猫？
2 马克买玩具熊猫花了多少钱？
3 阿曼达跟马克他们一起回宾馆吗？

售货员：你们好！ 进来看一看吧。
马克：小姐，这个熊猫多少钱？
售货员：很便宜，七十块。
马克：太贵了，可以便宜一点儿吗？
售货员：好吧，那就便宜一点儿。五十块怎么样？
阿曼达：我们是学生，钱不多。再便宜一点儿吧。三十块好不好？
售货员：你们真会讲价。三十块卖给你吧。
马克：谢谢。永民，你觉得王玉会喜欢这个熊猫吗？
永民：她一定喜欢！但是你怎么带回去呢？我们的行李已经太多了。
阿曼达：还是邮寄吧。宾馆附近有邮局。我还想给家人寄明信片呢。
售货员：你们是第一次来成都吗？普通话说得不错啊。
马克：你的普通话也很好啊！你说我们的韩国朋友应该买什么纪念品？

售货员：这件唐装怎么样？颜色很好看，很有中国味道。
永民：我可以试一试吗？
售货员：没问题。这件唐装是真丝的，穿着很舒服。
阿曼达：很帅啊！马克、永民，我想去那边看看，我们一会儿在宾馆见。
马克和永民：好，一会儿见！

［在邮局］
马克：麻烦您，我想寄这个包裹到北京。
工作人员：你需要填这张表。你看得懂吗？
马克：没问题。……填完了，给你。
工作人员：先称一下重量。……一点二公斤，平邮十一元，EMS二十七元。
马克：平邮多长时间？EMS多长时间？
工作人员：平邮两个星期左右，EMS三天就到。
马克：我寄EMS，给你钱。
工作人员：三十元，找你三元。
马克：谢谢，再见。

63

3 Listen again and complete the sentences.

1 售货员说他们很会 ________。
2 马克买的熊猫便宜了 _____ 元。
3 邮局在宾馆的 ________。
4 永民试穿的唐装是 _______ 的。
5 EMS比平邮快 ________ 天。

4 Work in pairs. Act out the conversation.

A: You work at a post office.
B: You want to send one of the following items from the post office.

1 唐装：寄去日本，0.5公斤，平邮108元，EMS180元
2 茶具：寄去澳大利亚，1公斤，平邮90元，EMS265元

Now change roles.

New words

jiǎngjià 讲价	bargain	pǔtōnghuà 普通话	Putonghua	bāoguǒ 包裹	parcel, package
mài 卖	sell	jìniànpǐn 纪念品	souvenir	biǎo 表	form, table
yídìng 一定	definitely, for sure	tángzhuāng 唐装	garment in a traditional Chinese style	dǒng 懂	understand
xíngli 行李	luggage	wèidào 味道	taste, feel (of clothes)	zhòngliàng 重量	weight
yóujì 邮寄	send by post	zhēnsī 真丝	real silk	gōngjīn 公斤	kilogram
míngxìnpiàn 明信片	postcard	yíhuìr 一会儿	a little while	píngyóu 平邮	ordinary post, surface mail

Pronunciation and speaking

The finals: "ian" and "üan"

64

1 Check the correct finals for the characters.

1 便 ☐ ian ☐ üan
2 园 ☐ ian ☐ üan
3 点 ☐ ian ☐ üan
4 钱 ☐ ian ☐ üan

Now listen and repeat.

65

2 Check the correct finals for the underlined characters.

1 便宜 ☐ ian ☐ üan
2 一点儿 ☐ ian ☐ üan
3 明信片 ☐ ian ☐ üan
4 问卷 ☐ ian ☐ üan
5 纪念品 ☐ ian ☐ üan
6 医院 ☐ ian ☐ üan

Now listen and repeat.

66

3 Say the sentences aloud.

Túshūguǎn de qiánbian yǒu jǐ gè yǎnyuán
1 图书馆 的 前边 有 几 个 演员。

Wǒ xiǎng zuò zhìyuànzhě huòzhě yùndòngyuán
2 我 想 做 志愿者 或者 运动员。

Wáng Yù zài gōngyuán ménkǒu tián wènjuàn
3 王 玉 在 公园 门口 填 问卷。

Mǎ Yuán mǎi de jìniànpǐn hěn piányi
4 马 园 买 的 纪念品 很 便宜。

Now listen and repeat.

67

4 Listen and say the words and expressions.

1 jìniànpǐn 纪念品 wánjù 玩具 míngxìnpiàn 明信片
2 wèidào 味道 zhēnsī 真丝 shūfu 舒服 hǎokàn 好看
3 Tài guì le 太贵了! Piányi yìdiǎnr ba 便宜一点儿吧。

5 Work in pairs.

A: Find five items in your bag that you would like to sell, and decide the price of each item.
B: Choose three items you would like to buy from A, and bargain for the lowest possible price for each one.

Now change roles.

CHINESE TO GO

68

Shopping expressions

Zhège zěnme mài 这个 怎么 卖?	How much is this?
Shí kuài qián yì jīn 十 块 钱 一 斤。	Ten yuan per 500 grams.
Kěyǐ dǎzhé ma 可以 打折 吗?	Can you give any discount?
Dǎ qī zhé 打 七 折。	30% off.
Yǒu yōuhuì ma 有 优惠 吗?	Is there a special offer?
Mǎi yī sòng yī 买 一 送 一。	Buy one, get one free.

LESSON 2

Reading and writing

1 Match the nouns with the appropriate descriptions.

1	gǎnjué 感觉	a	hěn dìdao 很 地道
2	yàngzi 样子	b	hěn piàoliang 很 漂亮
3	chájù 茶具	c	shūfu 舒服
4	chuāncài 川菜	d	hěn shuài 很 帅

69

2 Read Amanda's email to Wang Yu about her visit to Chengdu.

New words

zuótiān 昨天	yesterday	suǒyǒu 所有	all
jiā 家	(used for families or organizations)	guāng 光	used up, all gone
lǎo 老	old	yàngzi 样子	appearance
dìdao 地道	typical, authentic	tào 套	set
diǎn 点	order	chájù 茶具	tea set
yuè 越	more	qízhōng 其中	among
bù dé bù 不得不	have no choice but to/so you have to	gàosu 告诉	tell
gǎnjué 感觉	feel, feeling	zhù hǎo 祝 好	best wishes
pà 怕	be afraid, fear		

邮件转移至　确认　删除

邮箱 | 通讯录 | 相册 | 邮箱设置 | 帮助

王玉：

你好！

我和马克、永民已经到成都了。成都有很多好玩儿的景点，我们都玩得很开心。昨天晚上我们去了市中心附近的一家饭馆吃饭，饭馆的名字叫"老成都"，听说那里的川菜很地道。我们点了麻婆豆腐、宫保鸡丁，还有水煮鱼。开始吃的时候觉得味道很好，但是越吃越辣，最后我不得不喝了一大杯水，才感觉好一些。不过，马克和永民不怕辣，所有的菜很快就吃光了。

今天下午我们去市场买东西，那里的东西又多又便宜。永民买了一件唐装，他穿唐装的样子很帅。我看到这套茶具和这条围巾，很漂亮，我想买其中的一件送给你妈妈。你能告诉我你妈妈喜欢茶具还是围巾吗？

祝好！

阿曼达

发送

3 Choose the correct answers to the questions.

1 What is the second paragraph mainly about?

☐ a 吃川菜

☐ b 喝水

☐ c 到成都

2 What is the main idea of the third paragraph?

☐ a 市场的东西又多又便宜

☐ b 永民穿唐装的样子

☐ c 买茶具还是围巾

4 Read again and check the true statements.

☐ 1 "老成都" 离市中心很近。

☐ 2 阿曼达不怕辣。

☐ 3 她不喜欢永民穿唐装的样子。

☐ 4 她想买东西送给王玉的妈妈。

5 Write an email to a friend about a recent shopping experience. Make sure you mention

- the time and place
- what happened
- your feelings about it.

Use Amanda's email in Activity 2 to help you.

Language in use

Duplication of verbs

1 Look at the sentences.

Subject	Modal verb	Verb phrase	Object
		听听	音乐吧。
		看一看吧。	
我	可以	试一试吗?	

Now check the two correct explanations.

☐ 1 The duplication of verbs is used to soften your tone when making suggestions or requests.

☐ 2 The duplication of verbs creates a more forceful tone in suggestions or requests.

☐ 3 一 can be added between the duplicated verbs to express a mild tone.

2 Write the sentences in Chinese, using duplicated verbs.

1 Can you talk a bit about the history of Sydney?

2 I would like to have a walk in the park.

3 You should take a look at this book.

"The more... the more..." 越……越……

1 Look at the sentences.

Subject	越	Verb/ Adjective	越	Verb phrase/ Adjective phrase
我	越	吃	越	想吃。
马克	越	走	越	快。
她	越	想	越	不开心。
人	越	多	越	好。

Now check the two correct explanations.

☐ 1 越……越…… is used to indicate that one thing increases as something else continues or increases.

☐ 2 越 can be followed by a verb or an adjective.

☐ 3 Words linked by 越……越…… must be of the same part of speech.

2 Write sentences using 越……越…… and the given words.

1 他/长/高
2 我/说/高兴
3 她/跑/热

Notional passive

1 Look at the sentences.

Topic	Comment		
	Adverbial	Verb	Complement
表		填	完了。
所有的菜	很快就	吃	光了。
他的作业	还没有	写。	
钱	没	用	光。
书		放	在家里了。

Now check the two correct explanations.

☐ 1 In a notional passive sentence, no passive marker such as 被 is used, even though the doer of the action is not stated.

☐ 2 Notional passive is only used when the doer of the action is not known in the context.

☐ 3 The particle 了 is used in a positive sentence, but not in a negative sentence with 没.

2 Write the sentences in Chinese, using notional passive.

1 My homework is finished.
2 The clothes have not been washed yet.
3 All the souvenirs have sold out.
4 The coat is not ready yet.

Turn to page 166 for grammar reference.

LESSON | 3

Communication activity

1 Work in two groups.

Group A: You are souvenir sellers. Look at the souvenirs, and decide a price for each item.
Group B: You have a budget of 200 yuan to buy three souvenirs.

2 Imagine you are at the market. Group A stand at different "stalls" (desks) around the classroom. Group B walk around the "market".

Group A: Offer the souvenirs to customers, and bargain for the best price with them. Give reasons for your price if necessary. For example,

- 质量很好 good quality
- 颜色很漂亮 pretty colour
- 很有中国味道 very Chinese
- 很便宜 very cheap

Group B: Bargain for the best price for the items you want to buy. Give reasons for a lower price. For example,

- 不太好 not very good
- 不够漂亮 not pretty enough
- 太贵了 too expensive

3 Work with the whole class. Find out who made the most money and who got the best deals.

Turn to pages 150 and 156 for more speaking practice.

Cultural corner

Teahouses in Chengdu and *Longmen Zhen*

Teahouses are popular in many areas of China. Teahouses function as entertainment centres, community centres and as places for get-togethers and even business meetings. The city of Chengdu boasts a unique teahouse culture. You can find teahouses everywhere in Chengdu. People in the city, especially the elderly, not only enjoy drinking tea there, but also spend hours chatting, playing games, reading newspapers, eating snacks, and listening to storytellers. Chatting in a teahouse is known as *Longmen Zhen* (龙门阵). The word has its origins in the Tang Dynasty, when a general named Xue Rengui (薛仁贵) invented a battle formation called *Longmen Zhen*. The name implies that every teahouse in Chengdu is like a battlefield, bustling with endless activity!

Character writing

These are two common radicals in Chinese. Do you know any other characters with the same radicals?

Radical	Meaning	Examples
走	walk	走、超
刂	knife	剧、别

1 Look at the characters and identify the radicals.

刻　赵　刷　赶

2 Match the words with the meanings.

1 拿到
2 起床
3 越……越……
4 牙刷

a toothbrush
b the more... the more...
c get up
d get, take to

3 Trace the characters in the boxes.

起
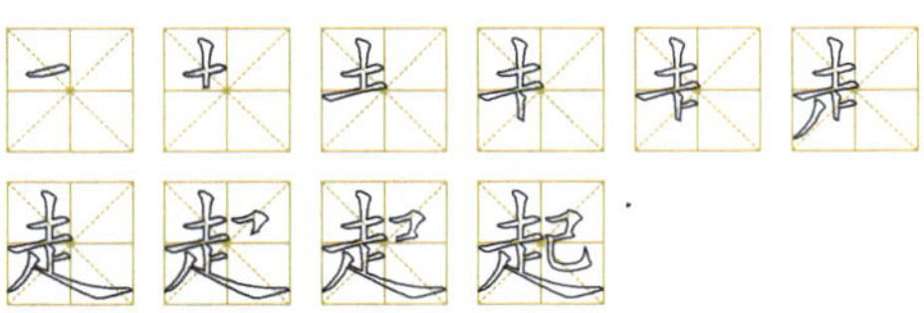

越
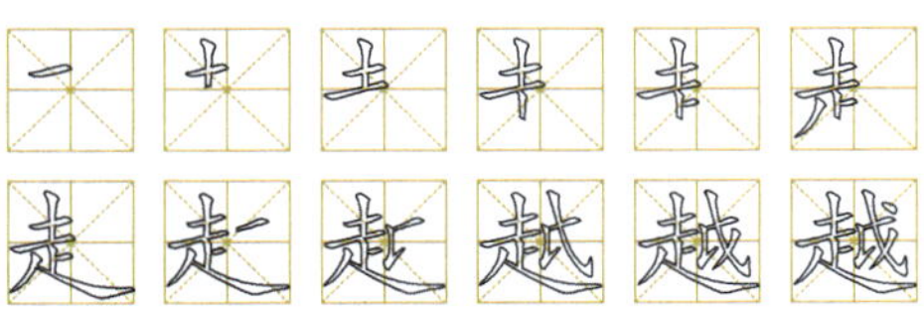

到
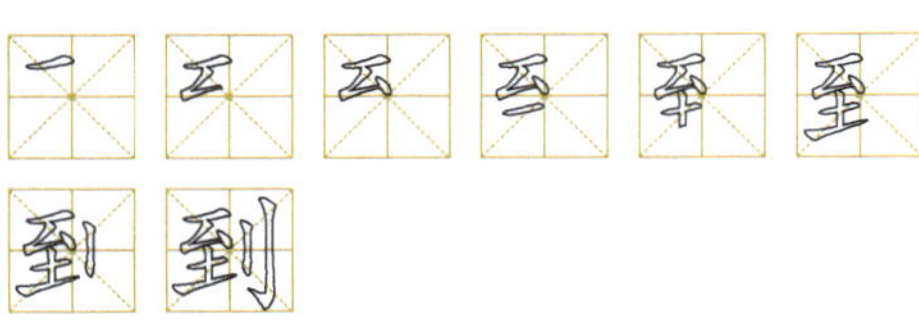

刷
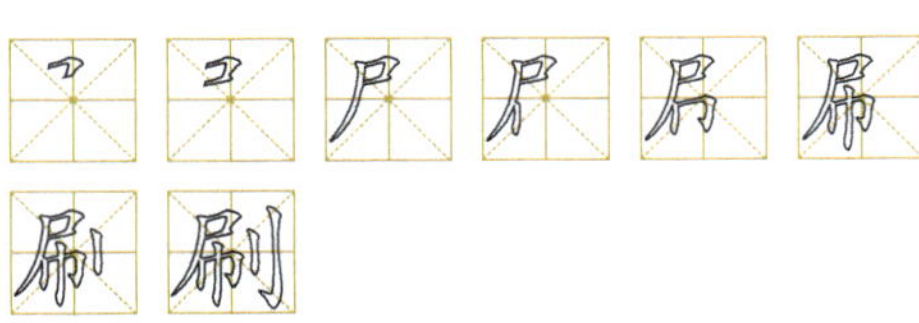

Review and practice

1 Put the sentences in the correct order to make a conversation.

a 太贵了，可以便宜一点儿吗？
b 太少了。一百块吧。
c 这件衣服多少钱？
d 再便宜一点儿吧。九十块，怎么样？
e 一百八。
f 那好吧。给你钱。
g 一百五卖给你吧。

2 Work in pairs. Take turns to make three suggestions with the given verbs, using a softened tone.

1 试　2 用　3 看

3 Rewrite the sentences using notional passive.

1 所有的菜都被他们吃光了。
2 马克填完了这张表。
3 小王准备好行李了。

4 Write two sentences to describe each picture, using 越……越…….

a

b

Vocabulary extension

Match the words with the objects in the picture.

1 pídài 皮带	2 shǒubiǎo 手表	3 lǐngdài 领带
4 qiánbāo 钱包	5 píxié 皮鞋	6 jìshìběn 记事本

Now work in pairs. Ask and answer questions about how much you have paid for these items.

Vocabulary review

Fill in the blanks.

包裹	bāoguǒ	*n.*	parcel, package
表	biǎo	*n.*	______
不得不	bù dé bù		have no choice but to/so you have to
茶具	chájù	*n.*	______
地道	dìdao	*adj.*	______
______	diǎn	*v.*	order
______	dǒng	*v.*	understand
感觉	gǎnjué	*v./n.*	______
______	gàosu	*v.*	tell
______	gōngjīn	*measure word*	kilogram
光	guāng	*adj.*	used up, all gone
纪念品	jìniànpǐn	*n.*	______
______	jiā	*measure word*	(used for families or organizations)
讲价	jiǎngjià	*v.*	______
______	lǎo	*adj.*	old
______	mài	*v.*	sell
明信片	míngxìnpiàn	*n.*	______
______	pà	*v.*	be afraid, fear
平邮	píngyóu	*v.*	ordinary post, surface mail
普通话	pǔtōnghuà	*n.*	______
其中	qízhōng	*n.*	______

______	suǒyǒu	*adj.*	all
唐装	tángzhuāng	*n.*	garment in a traditional Chinese style
套	tào	*n.*	set
味道	wèidào	*n.*	______
行李	xíngli	*n.*	______
样子	yàngzi	*n.*	appearance
______	yídìng	*adv.*	definitely, for sure
一会儿	yíhuìr	*n.*	______
邮寄	yóujì	*v.*	send by post
越	yuè	*adv.*	more
真丝	zhēnsī	*n.*	real silk
重量	zhòngliàng	*n.*	______
祝好	zhù hǎo		best wishes
______	zuótiān	*n.*	yesterday
记事本	jìshìběn	*n.*	notebook
领带	lǐngdài	*n.*	tie
毛笔	máobǐ	*n.*	Chinese writing brush
皮带	pídài	*n.*	leather belt
皮鞋	píxié	*n.*	leather shoe
钱包	qiánbāo	*n.*	wallet
手表	shǒubiǎo	*n.*	watch
玩具	wánjù	*n.*	toy

Review 2

Vocabulary

1 Match the activities with the places where they happen.

1 买票	a 市场
2 讲价	b 饭馆
3 登记入住	c 售票处
4 点菜	d 博物馆
5 参观文物	e 宾馆

2 Complete the phrases with the correct measure words.

1 一 ____ 衣柜	2 两 ____ 米饭
3 一 ____ 被子	4 三 ____ 汽水
5 一 ____ 毛巾	6 三 ____ 筷子
7 两 ____ 门票	8 一 ____ 唐装

3 Write three sentences to describe where the furniture is.

4 Write five sentences to describe what you usually do in the morning.

Grammar

1 Put the words in brackets in the correct places to complete the sentences.

1 你可以被子拿出来吗？（把）

2 我的书小王拿走了。（被）

3 他家的门口挂红灯笼。（着）

4 我的房间有三米，两米。（长/宽）

2 Write questions for the answers.

1 A：________________________？

B：古城墙有六百多年的历史。

2 A：________________________？

B：我奶奶已经八十多岁了。

3 A：________________________？

B：从北京到香港坐飞机要三个多小时。

4 A：________________________？

B：因为海外的中国人称他们自己为唐人。

5 A：________________________？

B：这个兵马俑有两米高。

3 Complete the sentences with the words in the box.

虽然	越……越……	所以	够

1 他昨天回家了，_____没有参加派对。

2 这个宾馆的床_____大，有两米宽。

3 马克的中文 _____ 说 _____ 好。

4 _____ 这里的麻婆豆腐很好吃，但是我不舒服，不能吃辣的。

4 Make sentences using the given words.

1 桌子/衣柜/旁边

2 被子/不够/暖和

3 衣服/洗/好

4 兵马俑/发现/农民

5 冬天/很冷/穿大衣

6 因为……所以……

7 指示牌/安静/着

8 筷子/放/桌子/把

9 公园/走一走

10 是……的

11 被/这本书/借

12 体育场/长/宽

5 Write a sentence to describe each picture using 把.

a

b

c

d

Now rewrite your sentences using 被.

Integrated skills

70

1 Listen and choose the correct answers to the questions.

1 他什么时候去吃川菜了？

a 今天　　b 昨天

2 她买了什么？

a 一条围巾　　b 一套茶具

3 他觉得麻婆豆腐的味道怎么样？

a 太辣了　　b 很好吃

4 她点了什么？

a 炒饭　　b 可乐

5 中文故事书在哪里？

a 桌子的旁边　　b 书柜的最上面

6 宾馆的服务怎么样？

a 很舒服　　b 不够好

7 房子的门口挂着什么？

a 指示牌　　b “不得进入”

8 平邮比EMS慢多少？

a 两天　　b 五天

2 Work in pairs. Put the sentences in the correct order to make a conversation.

a 很好玩儿。成都有很多好玩儿的景点。

b 你最喜欢哪个景点？

c 很好。我们已经去过西安，现在我们在成都。

d 对了，你们吃川菜了吗？

e 西安怎么样？

f 很不错。到了西安，才感觉到这里是真正的历史古城。

g 你们参观了什么景点？

h 我最喜欢兵马俑。那些兵马俑看起来像真的一样！

i 成都好玩儿吗？

j 吃过了。川菜又麻又辣，很好吃，但是我怕辣，不能吃太多。

k 阿曼达，你们的旅游怎么样？

l 我们参观了兵马俑、古城墙、钟楼和陕西历史博物馆。

The correct order is ____________________

3 **Write five sentences to describe the locations of the rooms in the flat, using 有/是, 旁边 and 对面.**

4 **Work in pairs. Write a conversation of six sentences for the people in each picture.**

a

b

Now act out the conversations.

Enjoy Chinese

Guess what these ancient Chinese characters resemble.

1		a	草
2		b	木
3		c	又
4		d	口
5		e	大
6		f	耳

Now match the ancient characters with the modern ones.

UNIT 9

Zhèli de fēngjǐng měi jí le
这里的风景美极了！

The scenery here is amazing!

LESSON | 1

Vocabulary and listening

71

1 Look at the picture below and check the things that you can find in it.

☐ hú 湖	☐ lántiān 蓝天
☐ shān 山	☐ shítou 石头
☐ niǎo 鸟	☐ shùmù 树木

Now listen and say the words.

72

2 Mark, Yeong-min and Amanda are at Jiuzhaigou Valley. Listen to the conversation and answer the questions.

1 为什么马克说“书店应该退钱”？

2 马克喜欢这个地方吗？永民呢？

马克：今天天气真好。

永民：这里的风景美极了！

阿曼达：是啊。这个湖特别漂亮。

永民：看，湖水刚才是蓝色的，现在变成了绿色。

马克：旅游书上说这个湖叫“五彩池”，应该有五种颜色啊。我现在只看到蓝色和绿色两种。书店应该退钱！

阿曼达：哈哈，真好笑。那边的湖水有很多种颜色，看到了吗？

马克：看到了！蓝天、白云、五彩的湖水和绿色的山，真美。

阿曼达：像一幅画。

马克：我很喜欢这种自然风景。这里的山特别美，和澳大利亚的山完全不一样。

永民：和韩国的山也不一样，很特别。我第一次看到这种山水。

阿曼达：我也喜欢这里，空气好，又安静。听到了吗？鸟儿在唱歌。

马克：哈哈，没错儿。在城市里听不到。

永民：看，这是我拍的照片。你们觉得怎么样？

阿曼达：不错。给我们照张相吧。

永民：没问题。一二三，笑一笑。

New words

fēngjǐng 风景	scenery	tuì qián 退钱	refund
měi jí le 美极了	amazing	hǎoxiào 好笑	funny
měi 美	beautiful	shān 山	mountain, hill
hú 湖	lake	huà 画	picture
tèbié 特别	especially, particularly	zìrán 自然	nature
gāngcái 刚才	just now, a moment ago	wánquán 完全	completely
biànchéng 变成	change into	shānshuǐ 山水	scenery with hills and water
lǚyóu 旅游	travel	niǎo 鸟	bird
cǎi 彩	colour	méicuòr 没错儿	be sure
chí 池	pond, pool	búcuò 不错	not bad
zhǒng 种	kind, type	zhàoxiàng 照相	take a photo

72

3 **Listen again and check the true statements.**

☐ 1 "五彩池"的湖水只有蓝和绿两种颜色。

☐ 2 阿曼达不喜欢听到鸟叫。

☐ 3 永民拍的照片很漂亮。

☐ 4 永民让阿曼达给他拍照。

4 **Work in pairs. Look carefully at the picture. You have 30 seconds to memorise as many details as possible.**

Now close your book. Describe the picture to your partner from memory and see who gets the most correct details.

Pronunciation and speaking

Difference between "j" and "z"

73

1 Check the correct initials for the characters.

1 在 ☐ j ☐ z
2 叫 ☐ j ☐ z
3 就 ☐ j ☐ z
4 怎 ☐ j ☐ z
5 最 ☐ j ☐ z

Now listen and repeat.

74

2 Check the correct initials for the underlined characters.

1 风<u>景</u> ☐ j ☐ z
2 美<u>极</u>了 ☐ j ☐ z
3 房<u>子</u> ☐ j ☐ z
4 看<u>见</u> ☐ j ☐ z
5 <u>自</u>然 ☐ j ☐ z
6 <u>几</u>个 ☐ j ☐ z

Now listen and repeat.

75

3 Read the sentences aloud.

1 Zhèli de fēngjǐng měi jí le
这里的风景美极了！

2 Zhè tào fángzi yǒu jǐ gè fángjiān
这套房子有几个房间？

3 Wǒ zuótiān zǒulù qù xuéxiào
我昨天走路去学校。

4 Nàge jìzhě zǒu jìn le zuǒbian de fángjiān
那个记者走进了左边的房间。

5 Chūnjié shì Hànzúrén zuì zhòngyào de jiérì
春节是汉族人最重要的节日。

Now listen and repeat.

76

4 Listen and say the words.

1 zìrán 自然 fēngjǐng 风景 huà 画 shānshuǐ 山水
2 tèbié 特别 yīnggāi 应该 wánquán 完全 gāngcái 刚才
3 zhàoxiàng 照相 ānjìng 安静 méicuòr 没错儿 biànchéng 变成

5 Complete the table with information about a beautiful place you have visited.

在哪里	
山水的特点	

我觉得________________

Now work in pairs. Ask and answer questions about the places you have chosen.

CHINESE TO GO

77

Questions to ask a tour guide

Xíngchéng shì zěnme ānpái de 行程是怎么安排的？	What's the itinerary?
Háiyǒu duō yuǎn 还有多远？	How far away is it?
Zài zhèli dāi duō jiǔ 在这里待多久？	How long are we going to stay here?
Kěyǐ zìyóu huódòng ma 可以自由活动吗？	Can I look around by myself?
Jǐ diǎn / Zài nǎr jíhé 几点/在哪儿集合？	What time/Where do we meet up?
Yǒu shénme tèchǎn 有什么特产？	What special local products are there?

LESSON 2

Reading and writing

1 **Work in pairs. Check the things you would expect to find at a nature reserve.**

☐ gāoshān 高山	☐ sēnlín 森林
☐ pùbù 瀑布	☐ shùmù 树木
☐ héliú 河流	☐ lántiān 蓝天
☐ húpō 湖泊	☐ báiyún 白云

78

2 **Read the flyer about the Wolong Reserve and Jiuzhaigou Valley.**

New words

bǎohùqū 保护区	conservation area	pùbù 瀑布	waterfall
wèiyú 位于	be located	sēnlín 森林	forest
zhàn 占	make up	fēicháng 非常	very, extremely
zǒngshù 总数	total number	rénjiān 人间	(human) world, the earth
bǎifēnzhī 百分之	percent	xiānjìng 仙境	paradise
xiāng 乡	hometown, countryside	qīngchè 清澈	clear
chú le 除了……	in addition, besides	dǐ 底	bottom
yǐwài 以外		shùmù 树木	tree
bǎohù 保护	protect	dàoyìng 倒映	reflect, mirror
zhíwù 植物	plant	jīchǎng 机场	airport

卧龙保护区

卧龙保护区位于成都的西北，离成都大约一百三十公里。保护区里有一百多只大熊猫，占全国总数的百分之十，所以被称为“熊猫之乡”。

除了大熊猫以外，保护区里还有很多其他受国家保护的动物和植物。

交通　旅游客车（成都—卧龙）3小时

九寨沟

九寨沟离成都四百多公里。这里的雪山、瀑布、湖泊和森林非常漂亮，被称为“人间仙境”。

九寨沟里有一百多个大大小小的湖泊。其中的五彩池清澈见底，蓝天、白云和树木倒映在水中，五颜六色，美极了。九寨沟里还有很多瀑布，其中最宽的瀑布宽两百多米，高二十多米。

交通　飞机（成都—九黄机场）1小时
旅游客车（成都—九寨沟）10小时

3 **Check the true statements.**

☐ 1 保护区里的动植物受国家保护。
☐ 2 从成都到卧龙坐旅游客车要三个小时。
☐ 3 九寨沟比较远，但是可以坐飞机去。
☐ 4 九寨沟里有一百多个瀑布。

4 **Read the flyer again and complete the table.**

	卧龙保护区	九寨沟
在哪里		
被称为		
特点		
交通		

Now work in pairs. Discuss and decide which place you would like to visit together.

我想去 __________ 旅游，因为……

5 **Design a travel flyer for a place you know well. Include where it is, what there is to see, how to get there and why it is special.**

Language in use

Indicating the result of an action with 到

1 **Look at the sentences.**

Subject	Adverbial	Verb	到	Object
我	第一次	看	到	这种山水。
你		找	到	书了吗？
马克		买	（不）到	火车票。

Now check the two correct explanations.

☐ 1 到 is used after a verb to indicate the result of an action.
☐ 2 A noun or noun phrase serving as the object must always be used after 到 to say what or who was involved in the action.
☐ 3 不 is used before the verb to indicate a negative result.

2 **Complete the sentences, using 到 and the given words.**

1 __________，你可以大声一点儿吗？（听）
2 你妈妈来学校了，__________？（见）
3 __________，你可以帮一下我吗？（找）

Expressing percentages using 百分之……

1 Look at the sentences.

Subject	Verb	Adjective phrase	Percentage
这里的熊猫数量	占	全国总数的	百分之十。
中文作业	占	（所有作业的）	百分之三十。
他的朋友	占	（派对人数的）	百分之五十。

Now check the two correct explanations.

☐ 1 A percentage is expressed by adding the character for a number after 百分之.

☐ 2 The verb 占 is used before an adjective phrase to explain what something is a proportion of.

☐ 3 An adjective phrase must be used in a sentence expressing a percentage.

2 Write the sentences, using 百分之…… and the given words.

1 女学生/学校人数/百分之五十

2 玩游戏/你的时间/百分之三十

3 当地人/工作人员/百分之九十

除了……以外，还……

1 Look at the sentences.

除了……以外	Subject	还	Verb	Object
除了大熊猫以外，	这里	还	有	很多受国家保护的动物和植物。
除了报纸以外，	永民	还	买了	一些故事书。
除了购物以外，	她	还	喜欢	拍照。

Now check the two correct explanations.

☐ 1 除了……以外 means "in addition to" or "besides" when it is used together with 还.

☐ 2 除了……以外 means "except" when it is used together with 还.

☐ 3 The word after 除了 must express things of the same nature as the topic of the main clause after 还.

2 Complete the sentences.

1 除了 ________，我还喜欢 ________。

2 除了 ________，我每天还要 ________。

3 除了 ________，我们还一起 ________。

Turn to page 167 for grammar reference.

LESSON 3

Communication activity

1 Work in groups. You are the activity coordinators for a group of Chinese students visiting your school. You are planning a day trip for them to a place of natural beauty.

- Choose a destination and write a plan. Describe the natural features and why it is so beautiful.
- Prepare a presentation about your planned trip.

2 Give your presentation to the class.

Now vote for the best plan.

Turn to pages 151 and 157 for more speaking practice.

Cultural corner

Famous mountains in China

China has many scenic mountain regions, but some peaks are better known than others, and are among the most visited sites in the country.

There are two sets of holy mountains in China: one associated with Taoism and the other with Buddhism. The Four Sacred Mountains of Buddhism (中国佛教四大名山) are Mount Wutai (五台山), Mount Emei (峨眉山), Mount Jiuhua (九华山) and Mount Putuo (普陀山). These mountains are home to famous Buddhist monasteries and are major sites of pilgrimage.

Each of the Taoist "Five Great Mountains" (五岳) is associated with one of the traditional Chinese cardinal directions: Mount Taishan (泰山) with the east, Mount Huashan (华山) with the west, Mount Hengshan (衡山) in Hunan with the south, Mount Hengshan (恒山) in Shanxi with the north and Mount Songshan (嵩山) with the centre. Mount Taishan is therefore also known as the "East Great Mountain" (东岳), Mount Songshan as "Central Great Mountain" (中岳) and so on.

Mount Huangshan (黄山) in Anhui Province is noted for its natural beauty rather than religious significance, and ever since the Qin Dynasty it has been considered one of the most beautiful locations in China. A well-known saying goes: 五岳归来不看山，黄山归来不看岳 – "When you come back from the Five Great Mountains, you won't want to look at ordinary mountains any more. When you return from Mount Huangshan, you won't want to see the Five Great Mountains."

Character writing

These are two common radicals in Chinese. Do you know any other characters with the same radicals?

Radical	Meaning	Examples
寸	inch	寺、时
阝(left)	mound	院、阳

1 **Look at the characters and identify the radicals.**

对　导　阿　降

2 **Match the words with the meanings.**

1 除了	a tour guide
2 下降	b sorry
3 导游	c except
4 对不起	d descend

3 **Trace the characters in the boxes.**

对

导

除

降

Review and practice

1 **Circle the odd word out in each line.**

1 瀑布	森林	风景	雪山
2 保护	自然	变成	倒映
3 完全	特别	非常	植物
4 好笑	美	不错	位于

2 **Write three sentences to describe the picture.**

3 **Write three sentences that you might say about the picture above, using 看到, 想到 and 找到.**

4 **Write three sentences about your school or country using 百分之…….**

5 **Write three sentences about yourself using 除了……以外，还…….**

Vocabulary extension

Match the words with things in the picture.

a 海滩 (hǎitān)　　b 悬崖 (xuányá)

c 海水 (hǎishuǐ)　　d 海浪 (hǎilàng)

Now work in pairs. Talk about a place you know that has the above things/features.

Vocabulary review

Fill in the blanks.

百分之	bǎifēnzhī	*n.*	percent
保护	bǎohù	*v.*	______
保护区	bǎohùqū	*n.*	conservation area
______	biànchéng	*v.*	change into
不错	búcuò	*adj.*	not bad
彩	cǎi	*n.*	colour
池	chí	*n.*	______
除了……以外	chúle... yǐwài		in addition, besides
倒映	dàoyìng	*v.*	reflect, mirror
底	dǐ	*n.*	bottom
______	fēicháng	*adv.*	very, extremely
风景	fēngjǐng	*n.*	scenery
______	gāngcái	*n.*	just now, a moment ago
好笑	hǎoxiào	*adj.*	______
湖	hú	*n.*	lake
______	huà	*n.*	picture
______	jīchǎng	*n.*	airport
旅游	lǚyóu	*v.*	______
没错儿	méicuòr		______
______	měi	*adj.*	beautiful
美极了	měi jí le		amazing
______	niǎo	*n.*	bird
瀑布	pùbù	*n.*	______
清澈	qīngchè	*adj.*	clear
人间	rénjiān	*n.*	(human) world, the earth
______	sēnlín	*n.*	forest
______	shān	*n.*	mountain, hill
山水	shānshuǐ	*n.*	______
树木	shùmù	*n.*	______
特别	tèbié	*adv.*	especially, particularly
退钱	tuì qián		______
______	wánquán	*adv.*	completely
位于	wèiyú	*v.*	______
仙境	xiānjìng	*n.*	paradise
乡	xiāng	*n.*	hometown, countryside
占	zhàn	*v.*	make up
______	zhàoxiàng	*v.*	take a photograph
植物	zhíwù	*n.*	______
种	zhǒng	*measure word*	kind, type
______	zìrán	*n.*	nature
总数	zǒngshù	*n.*	______
海浪	hǎilàng	*n.*	sea wave
海水	hǎishuǐ	*n.*	seawater
海滩	hǎitān	*n.*	beach
河流	héliú	*n.*	river
石头	shítou	*n.*	stone
悬崖	xuányá	*n.*	overhanging cliff

UNIT 10

Tā zhǎng shénme yàngzi

她长什么样子？

What does she look like?

LESSON | 1

Vocabulary and listening

79

1 Work in pairs. Discuss which adjectives can be used to describe the people in the picture below.

	gèzi	gāo	ǎi	zhōngděng
1	个子：	高	矮	中等
	shēncái	pàng	shòu	miáotiao
2	身材：	胖	瘦	苗条
	tóufa	cháng	duǎn	
3	头发：	长	短	
		hēisè	hèsè	jīnsè
		黑色	褐色	金色

Now listen and say the words.

80

2 At the hotel, Amanda is talking about some new friends she has made. Listen to the conversation and answer the questions.

1 阿曼达一会儿要做什么？
2 为什么马克问她的新朋友长什么样子？
3 马克和永民会一起去酒吧吗？

阿曼达：我回来了！你们俩在做什么？
永民：我们在看电视。你买了什么纪念品？
阿曼达：我给家人买了一些丝巾和明信片。对了，我还认识了两个新朋友。
马克：真的？
阿曼达：我一会儿要去咖啡店跟她们见面。你们去不去？
永民：我不太想去，坐在这里看电视很舒服。
阿曼达：我的新朋友都是女孩。
永民：那个咖啡店在附近吗？
阿曼达：啊，现在你有兴趣了！咖啡店在宾馆后面，离这里很近，走路五分钟就到了。

New words

liǎ 俩	two (a fusion of 两 and 个)	tóufa 头发	hair
diànshì 电视	TV	yǎnjing 眼睛	eye
sījīn 丝巾	silk scarf	zhōngděng 中等	medium
duì le 对了	by the way, that's right	miáotiao 苗条	slim, slender
nǚhái 女孩	girl	lìng 另	other, another
xìngqù 兴趣	interest	duǎn 短	short (length)
zhǎng 长	grow, develop	ǎi 矮	short (height)
Déguó 德国	Germany	pàng 胖	plump, fat
liúxuéshēng 留学生	overseas student	zhòngyào 重要	important
jīnsè 金色	golden, blond(e)		

马克：你的新朋友长什么样子？

阿曼达：一个叫丽莎，是德国留学生。她有金色的长头发，蓝色的眼睛，中等个子，很苗条。另一个叫孙玉香，是上海人。她的头发比较短，个子不高不矮，她比丽莎胖一点儿。

马克：听起来很有趣，但是你还没说最重要的。

阿曼达：什么是重要的？

永民：马克最想知道她们漂亮不漂亮，还有她们有没有男朋友！

阿曼达：我要走了。如果你们想知道，就跟我来吧。

80

3 Listen again and check the true statements.

- ☐ 1 丽莎的个子不高也不矮。
- ☐ 2 丽莎比玉香瘦一点儿。
- ☐ 3 玉香的头发和丽莎的一样长。
- ☐ 4 永民想知道她们有没有男朋友。

4 Work in pairs.

A: Choose a person in the pictures on page 114 or 115 and answer B's questions.

B: Ask questions about the person's appearance and guess who it is.

Now change roles.

Pronunciation and speaking

The neutral tone

81

1 Look at the tone marks. How do they change?

1 xiǎngxiang 想想
2 kànkan 看看
3 shìshi 试试
4 shénme 什么
5 shuōshuo 说说
6 nǎli 哪里

Now listen and repeat.

82

2 Listen and check the pinyin with the tones you hear.

1 漂亮	☐	piàoliàng	☐	piàoliang
2 朋友	☐	péngyǒu	☐	péngyou
3 眼睛	☐	yǎnjīng	☐	yǎnjing
4 样子	☐	yàngzǐ	☐	yàngzi
5 头发	☐	tóufà	☐	tóufa

Now listen again and repeat.

83

3 Say the sentences aloud.

1 Nǐ de péngyou zhǎng shénme yàngzi
你的朋友长什么样子?

2 Tā hěn piàoliang, cháng tóufa, gāo gèzi
她很漂亮，长头发，高个子。

3 Wǒ kěyǐ shìshi zhè jiàn yīfu ma
我可以试试这件衣服吗?

4 Nǐ shuōshuo wǒ yīnggāi mǎi shénme
你说说我应该买什么?

5 Nǐ xiǎngxiang bǎ dōngxi fàng zài nǎli le
你想想把东西放在哪里了。

Now listen and repeat.

84

4 Listen and say the words.

1	yàngzi 样子	gèzi 个子	tóufa 头发	yǎnjing 眼睛
2	miáotiao 苗条	shòu 瘦	pàng 胖	ǎi 矮
3	jīnsè 金色	zhōngděng 中等	cháng 长	duǎn 短

5 Draw a picture of what you looked like when you were younger.

Now work in pairs. Describe how your partner's appearance has changed.

CHINESE TO GO

85

Expressions to describe appearance

Rén bù kě mào xiàng
人不可貌相。
Don't judge people by their appearances.

Tā zhǎng de hěn xiàng tā bàba
他长得很像他爸爸。
He looks a lot like his father.

Nǐ liǎ yìdiǎnr yě bú xiàng
你俩一点儿也不像。
You two don't look like each other at all.

Tā hǎo shuài gāo kě'ài
他好帅/高/可爱!
He is very handsome/tall/cute!

LESSON | 2

Reading and writing

1 Work in pairs. Describe the man's appearance and what he is wearing. Use the words below.

qiúyī 球衣	yùndòngkù 运动裤
qiúxié 球鞋	wàzi 袜子

New words

érqiě 而且	and, but also	yúkuài 愉快	happy, pleasant
tiāoxuǎn 挑选	choose	jiǔ 久	for a long time
gèng 更	more, even more	zuìjìn 最近	recently
qiúyī 球衣	jersey, team kit (for sports)	zhōnghào 中号	medium size
biǎodì 表弟	cousin (younger male)	Bāxī 巴西	Brazil
shòu 瘦	thin, skinny	shēncái 身材	figure, stature
wèntí 问题	question, problem	pífū 皮肤	skin

86

2 Read Wang Yu's emails to Amanda and her cousin in Chengdu.

邮件转移至 确认 删除

邮箱 | 通讯录 | 相册 | 邮箱设置 |

阿曼达：

知道你们已经到了成都，而且玩得很开心，我很高兴。我很想看看永民穿唐装的样子，一定很帅。你挑选的两件东西都很漂亮，我觉得我妈妈可能更喜欢茶具。

另外，谢谢你帮我带球衣给我表弟。明天晚上他会去你住的宾馆拿球衣。我表弟叫王明，十七岁，个子很高，比较瘦，短头发，戴眼镜。他的手机号码是16521659870。

如果你有问题，可以给我打电话。

祝旅行愉快！

王玉

发送

邮件转移至 确认 删除

邮箱 | 通讯录 | 相册 | 邮箱设置 |

小明：

好久不见，你最近好吗？你的生日就要到了，我让朋友从英国带回来一套球衣给你，是你最喜欢的那个球队的。球衣有蓝白两种颜色，我想你应该穿中号的，希望你喜欢。

我的朋友阿曼达去成都玩，我让她把球衣带给你。阿曼达是巴西人，个子不高，中等身材，黑皮肤，长头发。她住在成都宾馆，你可以明天晚上去宾馆找她，她的电话号码是16912764805。

祝生日快乐！

王玉

发送

3 **Check the true statements.**

☐ 1 王玉觉得永民穿唐装不好看。

☐ 2 王玉的表弟会去宾馆找阿曼达。

☐ 3 王玉让阿曼达从美国带球衣给表弟。

☐ 4 阿曼达没有见过王玉的表弟。

4 **Write four sentences, comparing the appearances of Amanda and Wang Yu's cousin.**

5 **Write a short description of what your best friend looks like.**

Now work in pairs. Listen to your partner's description and draw a picture of his/her friend.

Language in use

Serial verb constructions

1 **Look at the sentences.**

Subject	Predicate	
	Verb phrase 1	Verb phrase 2
我	去咖啡店	跟她们见面。
我	坐在这里	看电视。
我	买了一件球衣	送给你。
你	去宾馆	找她。
他们	坐火车	去成都。

Now check the two correct explanations.

☐ 1 A predicate can contain more than one verb phrase, describing consecutive actions.

☐ 2 The order of the verb phrases can be switched around without affecting the meaning.

☐ 3 The verb phrases are related in manner or purpose.

2 **Join the two sentences together, using serial verb constructions.**

1 我回家。/ 我吃晚饭。

2 我晚上去学校。/ 我上中文课。

3 我坐飞机。/ 我去听音乐会。

4 我每天早上到体育场。/ 我每天早上跑步。

Affirmative-negative questions

1 Look at the sentences.

Subject	Predicate	
	Adjective/Verb	Object
你们	去不去?	
Will you go or not?		
她们	漂亮不漂亮?	
Are they pretty or not?		
这件衣服	贵不贵?	
Is this piece of clothing expensive or not?		
你	买没买	那条裙子?
Have you bought that skirt?		
她	看没看	电影?
Has she seen the movie?		

Now check the two correct explanations.

☐ 1 Affirmative-negative questions are used to get straight yes or no answers.

☐ 2 These questions always contain a verb or an adjective and its negative form.

☐ 3 Affirmative-negative questions must contain the negative adverb 不.

2 Rewrite the sentences into affirmative-negative questions.

1 你明天去学校吗?
2 安娜买那件大衣了吗?
3 这个菜好吃吗?
4 你喜欢打网球吗?

Describing immediate actions with （就）要……了

1 Look at the sentences.

Subject	Adverb	Predicate
我	（就）要	走了。
你的生日	（就）要	到了。
我们	（就）要	去上海了。
她	（就）要	二十一岁了。

Now check the two correct explanations.

☐ 1 （就）要……了 is used to describe an action or event that is going to happen soon.

☐ 2 了 is used at the end of the sentence to indicate that something has happened.

☐ 3 就 can be left out, whereas 要 must be used.

2 Write the sentences in Chinese.

1 Will you go to Shanghai soon?
2 I'm going to the hospital tomorrow.
3 My mother is turning 60.
4 We're about to get off the train.
5 The summer holiday is coming.

Turn to page 168 for grammar reference.

LESSON 3

Communication activity

1 **Choose a student from the class and write five sentences to describe his/her appearance. For example,**

她是女的。
她个子不高。
她的头发是红色的。
她比我瘦。
她年纪和我一样大。

2 **Work in groups. Take turns to say the descriptions to the group one sentence at a time. Don't say the name of the student you are describing.**

Other students in the group guess who is being described. The winner is the person who makes the most correct guesses.

Turn to pages 151 and 157 for more speaking practice.

Cultural corner

Who is beautiful?

The standards of beauty have changed many times over the centuries in China, and the great beauties of one age might be considered quite plain in other eras.

In general, looks were considered more important for women than for men, since society permitted women few opportunities to distinguish themselves by other means in ancient times.

For women, in most eras, a slim, willowy figure was considered desirable. Zhao Feiyan, wife of the Han Emperor Cheng, was said to be so petite she could dance on the palm of a man's hand. She was often compared with Yang Yuhuan, the beautiful concubine of the Tang Emperor Xuanzong, because Zhao was known for her slender build while Yang was known for being rather plump. This is the source of the Chinese expression *yanshou huanfei* (燕瘦环肥), describing how people can differ, yet still be attractive.

Character writing

These are two common radicals in Chinese. Do you know any other characters with the same radicals?

Radical	Meaning	Examples
目	eye	看、睡
子	child	孙、好

1 **Look at the characters and identify the radicals.**

孩　省　睛　学

2 **Match the words with the meanings.**

1 女孩　　a watch TV
2 眼睛　　b girl
3 看电视　　c overseas student
4 留学生　　d eye

3 **Trace the characters in the boxes.**

看

眼
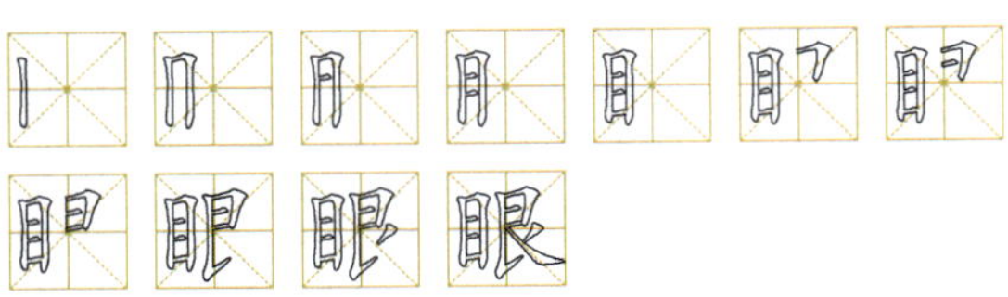

孩
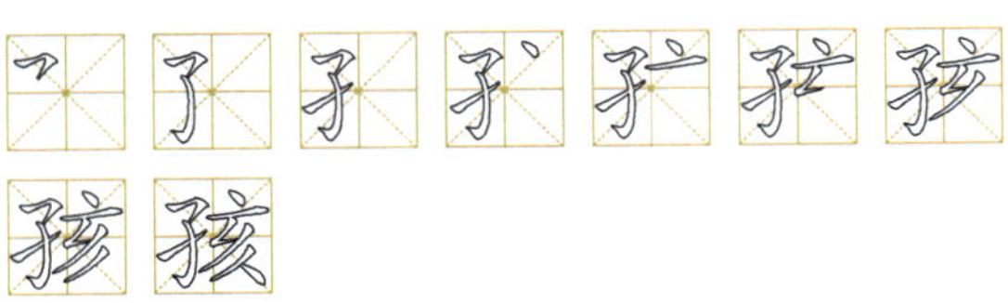

学
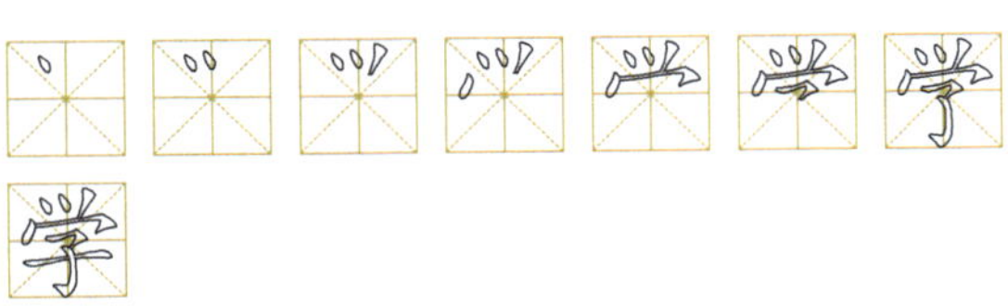

Review and practice

1 **Write sentences with the given phrases, using serial verb constructions.**

1 去英国/看足球比赛
2 坐地铁/上班
3 到市中心/找房子
4 买东西/送给朋友
5 到朋友家/庆祝生日

2 **Work in pairs. Ask and answer three affirmative-negative questions about each other.**

3 **Write five sentences to describe the appearances of the people in the picture, including their ages, heights, builds and hair.**

4 **Work in pairs. Talk about three things that are going to happen soon, using （就）要……了.**

Vocabulary extension

Match the words with the facial features of the man in the picture.

a 脸 (liǎn)	b 鼻子 (bízi)	c 嘴 (zuǐ)
d 耳朵 (ěrduo)	e 眉毛 (méimao)	f 胡子 (húzi)

Now work in pairs. Describe the man's appearance using these words. Discuss whether you think he is good-looking and explain why.

Vocabulary review

Fill in the blanks.

矮	ǎi	*adj.*	short (stature)
巴西	Bāxī	*n.*	Brazil
______	biǎodì	*n.*	cousin (younger male)
德国	Déguó	*n.*	______
______	diànshì	*n.*	TV
短	duǎn	*adj.*	______
______	duì le		by the way, that's right
而且	érqiě	*conj.*	and, but also
更	gèng	*adv.*	more, even more
金色	jīnsè	*n.*	golden, blond(e)
久	jiǔ	*adj.*	for a long time
俩	liǎ	*num.*	two (a fusion of 两 and 个)
另	lìng	*pron.*	other, another
______	liúxuéshēng	*n.*	overseas student
苗条	miáotiao	*adj.*	______
______	nǚhái	*n.*	girl
胖	pàng	*adj.*	______
皮肤	pífū	*n.*	skin
球衣	qiúyī	*n.*	jersey, team kit for sports
______	shēncái	*n.*	figure, stature
瘦	shòu	*adj.*	______
丝巾	sījīn	*n.*	silk scarf

挑选	tiāoxuǎn	*v.*	______
______	tóufa	*n.*	hair
______	wèntí	*n.*	question, problem
兴趣	xìngqù	*n.*	______
眼睛	yǎnjing	*n.*	eye
愉快	yúkuài	*adj.*	happy, pleasant
长	zhǎng	*v.*	______
中等	zhōngděng	*adj.*	medium
______	zhōnghào	*adj.*	medium size
重要	zhòngyào	*adj.*	______
最近	zuìjìn	*n.*	______
鼻子	bízi	*n.*	nose
耳朵	ěrduo	*n.*	ear
褐色	hèsè	*n.*	brown
胡子	húzi	*n.*	moustache
脸	liǎn	*n.*	face
眉毛	méimao	*n.*	eyebrow
球鞋	qiúxié	*n.*	sports shoe
袜子	wàzi	*n.*	sock
嘴	zuǐ	*n.*	mouth

UNIT 11

Wǒ juéde bù shūfu
我觉得不舒服。

I'm not feeling well.

LESSON | 1

Vocabulary and listening

87

1 Match the medicine labels with the meanings.

1 měi rì sān cì
每日三次

2 měi cì liǎng piàn
每次两片

3 fàn hòu fúyòng
饭后服用

4 yǐnqǐ shuìyì
引起睡意

a cause drowsiness
b three times a day
c take after meals
d two tablets each time

Now listen and say the phrases.

88

2 Work in pairs. Check the symptoms of a cold.

☐ tóutòng 头痛
☐ késou 咳嗽
☐ fāshāo 发烧
☐ hóulóng tòng 喉咙痛
☐ bísè 鼻塞
☐ lā dùzi 拉肚子

Now listen and say the words.

89

3 Back in Beijing, Mark goes to the doctor. Listen to the conversation and answer the questions.

1 马克得了什么病?
2 马克为什么病了?
3 马克的病应该怎么治?

医生：请坐！你叫什么名字？
马克：我叫马克。
医生：你觉得哪里不舒服？
马克：我有一点儿头痛，发烧，还拉肚子。
医生：多长时间了？
马克：两天了。
医生：你最近有没有离开过本地？
马克：有。我跟两个朋友去成都旅行，刚回来。
医生：先检查一下吧。张大嘴，让我看看你的喉咙。
马克：啊——
医生：再听听肺。
马克：医生，我得了什么病？

医生：没什么大问题，只是普通的感冒。你生病是因为没休息好，又着凉了。

马克：那应该怎么治？要打针吗？

医生：不用打针，我给你开一些药。好好休息，不要吃太辣的东西，很快就会好的。

马克：谢谢医生。

［在药房］

护士：马克，这是你的药。这是感冒和退烧药，每天三次，每次两片，饭前或者饭后服用都可以。请注意，吃药以后可能会想睡觉。

马克：谢谢你，再见。

New words

tóutòng 头痛	have a headache	xiūxi 休息	rest
fāshāo 发烧	have a fever	zháoliáng 着凉	catch a cold
lā dùzi 拉肚子	suffer from diarrhoea	zhì 治	treat (disease)
běndì 本地	this locality	dǎzhēn 打针	have/give an injection
jiǎnchá 检查	check up, examine	yào 药	medicine
hóulóng 喉咙	throat	hùshi 护士	nurse
fèi 肺	lung	tuìshāo 退烧	bring down a fever
débìng 得病	become ill	piàn 片	tablet
pǔtōng 普通	ordinary, common	fúyòng 服用	take (medicine)
gǎnmào 感冒	cold, catch a cold	zhùyì 注意	pay attention to
shēngbìng 生病	get sick		

89

4 Listen again and check the true statements.

☐ 1 马克病了两天了。

☐ 2 医生先听肺，然后检查喉咙。

☐ 3 马克的药只能饭后服用。

☐ 4 感冒药可能会让人想睡觉。

5 Complete the sentences.

1 马克有一点儿 ______，______，还 ______。

2 医生叫马克好好 ______，不要 ______。

3 马克的药每天要吃 ______ 次。

6 Work in pairs. Act out a conversation between a doctor and a patient who has got a stomach ache.

Pronunciation and speaking

Tone sandhi: 不 and 一

90

1 Look at the tone marks for 一 and 不. How do they change when the following character carries a fourth tone?

不用 búyòng	一片 yí piàn
不是 bú shì	一件 yí jiàn
不要 bú yào	一次 yí cì
不错 búcuò	一共 yígòng

How do they change when the following character carries other tones?

不舒服 bù shūfu	一些 yìxiē
不能 bù néng	一天 yì tiān
不来 bù lái	一年 yì nián
不好 bù hǎo	一点儿 yìdiǎnr

Now listen and repeat.

91

2 Write pinyin with the correct tones for the words.

1 一个 ____________________

2 一瓶 ____________________

3 不辣 ____________________

4 不咸 ____________________

Now listen and repeat.

92

3 Say the sentences aloud, using the correct tones.

1 Wǒ de tóu bú tòng le, búyòng chī yào le.
我的头不痛了，不用吃药了。

2 Wǒ zhīdào yì zhǒng yào, zhì gǎnmào búcuò.
我知道一种药，治感冒不错。

3 Wǒ bù zhīdào tā qù bú qù.
我不知道他去不去。

4 Yí gè píngguǒ hé yì bēi niúnǎi, duōshao qián?
一个苹果和一杯牛奶，多少钱？

Now listen and repeat.

93

4 Listen and say the words.

1	tóutòng 头痛	fāshāo 发烧	lādùzi 拉肚子	gǎnmào 感冒
2	débìng 得病	kànbìng 看病	chī yào 吃药	dǎzhēn 打针
3	xiūxi 休息	zháoliáng 着凉	tuìshāo 退烧	zhùyì 注意
4	jiǎnchá 检查	fúyòng 服用	kāi yào 开药	zhìbìng 治病

5 Work in pairs. Ask and answer questions about your last visit to the doctor.

CHINESE TO GO

94

Expressions related to sickness

Bìng cóng kǒu rù 病从口入。	Illness finds its way in by the mouth.
Nǐ de qìsè bú tài hǎo 你的气色不太好。	You don't look well.
Hǎo yìdiǎnr le ma 好一点儿了吗？	Are you feeling any better?
Duō bǎozhòng 多保重。	Take care.
Zǎorì kāngfù 早日康复。	Get well soon.

LESSON 2

Reading and writing

1 **Match the words with the pictures.**

hē shuǐ	chī shūcài	shuìjiào	yùndòng
1 喝水	2 吃蔬菜	3 睡觉	4 运动

Now work in pairs. Put the words in order of their importance for a healthy life.

95

2 **Read the poster and answer the questions.**

1 想健康地生活，应该做什么？

2 想健康地生活，不应该做什么？

New words

jiànkāng 健康	healthy, health	dìngshí 定时	at fixed times
shēnghuó 生活	life, live	dìngliàng 定量	with fixed quantity
chángshí 常识	general knowledge, common sense	ànshí 按时	on time
shēntǐ 身体	body	bǎo 饱	full, replete
de 地	(used with an adverb or adverbial phrase)	jīngcháng 经常	often
shūcài 蔬菜	vegetable	zhěngtiān 整天	whole day, all day
yán 盐	salt	wǎn 晚	late

你吃的东西健康吗？

要多吃蔬菜和水果，少吃多油、多盐的饭菜。

你的早、午、晚饭定时、定量吗？

要按时吃饭，早饭要吃好，午饭要吃饱，晚饭要吃少。

你每天喝的水够不够？

要多喝水，每天最少喝八杯水。

你经常做运动吗？

要多做运动，每天最好运动半个小时。不要整天在家看电视或上网玩电子游戏。

你每天睡觉的时间够吗？

要早睡早起，每天最少要睡八个小时。不要很晚才上床睡觉。

3 **Read again and complete the sentences.**

1 应该多吃 ________，少吃 ________。

2 早饭应该 ________，午饭应该 ________，晚饭应该 ________。

3 每天最少要喝 ________ 杯水。

4 每天最好做 ________ 个小时运动。

5 每天睡觉最少要 ________ 个小时。

4 **Work in pairs. Write five things you must or mustn't do in order to lead a healthy life.**

Language in use

The auxiliary word 地

1 **Look at the sentences.**

Subject	Modal verb	Adverbial phrase		Verb
人们	想	健康	地	生活。
她		高兴	地	回家了。
你	要	好好	地	休息。
他		慢慢	地	走了。

Now check the two correct explanations.

☐ 1 地 is used between an adjective and a verb to denote the manner of an action.

☐ 2 地 is used between a verb and its subject to denote the manner of an action.

☐ 3 地 cannot be used after the verb that the adverbial phrase describes.

2 **Make sentences using 地 and the given words.**

1 慢慢/吃着早餐

2 开心/唱着歌

3 很快/离开学校

4 愉快/去旅行

多 and 少

1 Look at the sentences.

Modal verb	多/少	Verb	Object
要	多	吃	水果和蔬菜。
	多	吃了	两碗饭。
要	多	喝	水。
要	多	做	运动。
	少	看	电视。
	少	写	一个字。

Now check the two correct explanations.

☐ 1 多 is used before a verb to mean doing something more, while 少 is used before a verb to mean doing something less.

☐ 2 多 or 少 can be used between the verb it modifies and the object to indicate a greater or lesser quantity.

☐ 3 When a verb is used with 多 or 少, the additional or lesser quantity can be specified by placing a number and measure word after the verb.

2 Work in pairs. Make two suggestions to each other, using 多 and 少 respectively.

Indicating the duration of an action

1 Look at the sentences.

Subject	Adverbial	Verb phrase	Verb	了	Duration
马克	每天	做运动	做		半个小时。
她	下午	打网球	打	了	两个小时。
永民	中午	吃饭	吃	了	十五分钟。
他			走	了	半个小时。

Now check the two correct explanations.

☐ 1 A noun phrase for the duration of an action is used at the end of the sentence.

☐ 2 When the verb phrase contains an object, it needs to be followed by a repetition of the verb.

☐ 3 了 must be used before the verb to indicate that something has already happened.

2 Write the sentences in Chinese.

1 I went shopping for three hours last Saturday.
2 He has been waiting for me for two hours.
3 She eats lunch for one hour every day.
4 Mark spent half an hour writing his blog last night.

Turn to page 169 for grammar reference.

LESSON 3

Communication activity

1 **Work in pairs. You are planning to write an article for a school newspaper about a common health problem. Brainstorm problems that you could write about.**

Now discuss and choose one problem to write about.

2 **Do research on the following questions, and then write the article based on your answers.**

生病时会有什么感觉？
为什么会得病？
什么人容易得这种病？
这种病怎么治？

3 **Work with another pair. Present your article to them and answer questions.**

Turn to pages 152 and 158 for more speaking practice.

Cultural corner

Traditional Chinese medicine

Not only does traditional Chinese medicine still have a big presence in China and in other Asian countries, it is also gaining popularity in the West as an alternative to some standard medical practices. The most well-known forms of Chinese medical treatment include the use of Chinese herbs, acupuncture, *tui na* massage and cupping. The underlying philosophy of Chinese medicine, upon which its models of the human body and its medical theories are built, is quite different from that of contemporary Western medicine. Chinese medicine treats the human body as a balanced system and views any specific illness as the result of that delicate balance being broken. Therefore, Chinese medicine aims at restoring that balance and focuses more on prevention than treatment. A traditional Chinese medicine practitioner uses four techniques for diagnosis, referred to as observation (望), listening and smelling (闻), asking (问), and touching and taking a pulse (切).

Character writing

These are two common radicals in Chinese. Do you know any other characters with the same radicals?

Radical	Meaning	Examples
疒	sickness	病、瘦
火	fire	焚、炒

1 Look at the characters and identify the radicals.

痛　疼　烧　烦

2 Match the words with the meanings.

1 得病　　a have a fever
2 发烧　　b have a headache
3 头痛　　c bother
4 麻烦　　d get sick

3 Trace the characters in the boxes.

病
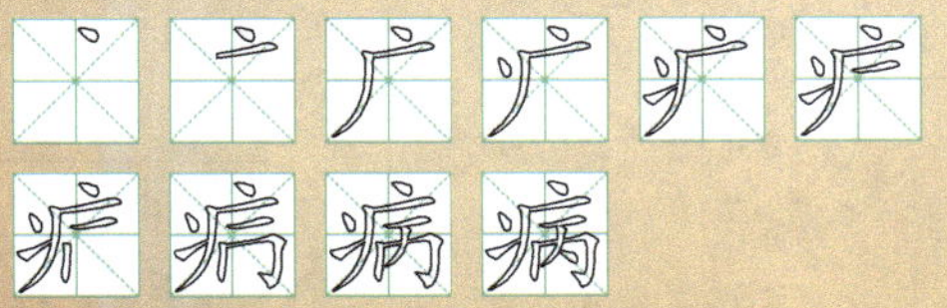

痛
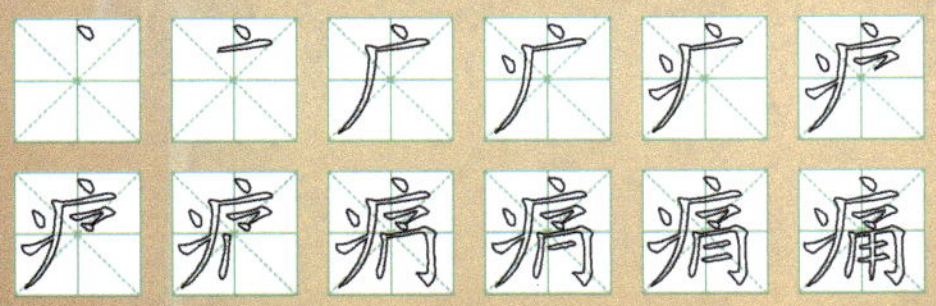

烧
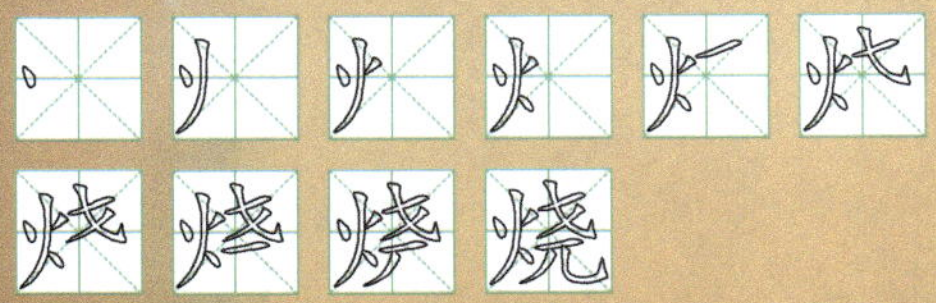

烦
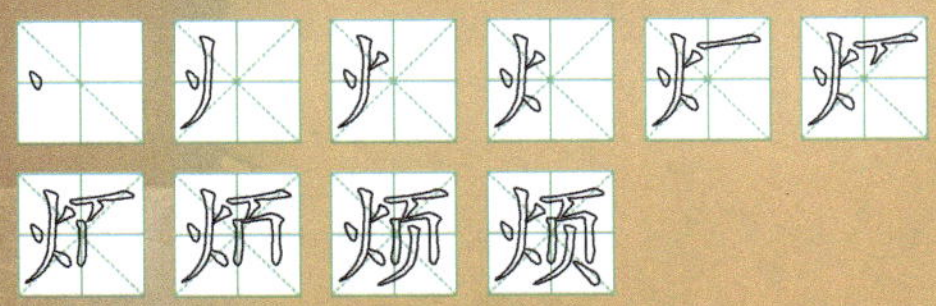

Review and practice

1 Circle the odd word out in each line.

1 头痛　检查　发烧　拉肚子
2 打针　吃药　休息　着凉
3 生活　身体　常识　经常
4 水果　饭菜　蔬菜　按时

2 Write sentences using 地 and the given words.

1 愉快/生活　　2 慢慢/停下
3 很快/走去　　4 开心/告诉

3 Write a sentence to describe each picture.

a

b

Now write two suggestions you would give to the people in the pictures.

4 Work in pairs. Tell each other how long you spent studying, sleeping and eating yesterday.

Vocabulary extension

Match the words for symptoms with the meanings.

1 dǎ pēntì 打喷嚏	a dizzy
2 liú bítì 流鼻涕	b stomach ache
3 ǒutù 呕吐	c have a sore throat
4 tóuyūn 头晕	d sneeze
5 sǎngzi téng 嗓子疼	e have a runny nose
6 dùzi tòng 肚子痛	f vomit

Now work in pairs. Tell each other when you had any of these symptoms before and try to explain why.

Vocabulary review

Fill in the blanks.

按时	ànshí	*adv.*	______
______	bǎo	*adj.*	full, replete
本地	běndì	*n.*	______
______	chángshí	*n.*	general knowledge, common sense
打针	dǎzhēn	*v.*	______
得病	débìng	*v.*	get sick
______	de	*particle*	(used with an adverb or adverbial phrase)
定量	dìngliàng	*v./n.*	with fixed quantity
______	dìngshí	*v./n.*	at fixed times
发烧	fāshāo	*v.*	______
肺	fèi	*n.*	lung
服用	fúyòng	*v.*	take (medicine)
______	gǎnmào	*n./v.*	cold, catch a cold
喉咙	hóulóng	*n.*	______
______	hùshi	*n.*	nurse
检查	jiǎnchá	*v.*	check up, examine
健康	jiànkāng	*adj./n.*	______
______	jīngcháng	*adv.*	often
拉肚子	lā dùzi		______
______	piàn	*measure word*	tablet
普通	pǔtōng	*adj.*	ordinary, common
______	shēntǐ	*n.*	body

生病	shēngbìng	*v.*	______
______	shēnghuó	*n./v.*	life, live
蔬菜	shūcài	*n.*	______
______	tóutòng	*v.*	have a headache
退烧	tuìshāo	*v.*	______
______	wǎn	*adj.*	late
______	xiūxi	*v.*	rest
盐	yán	*n.*	______
药	yào	*n.*	medicine
着凉	zháoliáng	*v.*	catch a cold
整天	zhěngtiān	*n.*	whole day, all day
______	zhì	*v.*	treat (disease)
注意	zhùyì	*v.*	______
鼻塞	bísè	*v.*	have a stuffy nose
打喷嚏	dǎ pēntì		sneeze
肚子痛	dùzi tòng		stomach ache
咳嗽	késou	*v.*	cough
流鼻涕	liú bítì		have a runny nose
呕吐	ǒutù	*v.*	vomit
嗓子疼	sǎngzi téng		have a sore throat
头晕	tóuyūn	*v.*	dizzy
引起睡意	yǐnqǐ shuìyì		cause drowsiness

UNIT 12

Nǐ huì xǐhuan tā de

你会喜欢她的！

You'll really like her!

LESSON 1

Vocabulary and listening

96

1 Work in pairs. Tell each other about your best friend's personality, using the words below.

xìnggé 性格	personality
píqi 脾气	temper, disposition
lèguān 乐观	optimistic
zìxìn 自信	self-confident
jí píqi 急脾气	hot temper
guānxīn 关心	caring

Now listen and say the words.

97

2 Wang Yu, Amanda and Mark are at a karaoke bar, chatting about a friend of Wang Yu's. Listen to the conversation and check the correct answers.

1 王玉的朋友凯特是 ________ 人。
- ☐ a 美国
- ☐ b 英国
- ☐ c 加拿大

2 凯特现在在北京 ________。
- ☐ a 工作
- ☐ b 学中文
- ☐ c 唱歌

3 阿曼达的性格 ________。
- ☐ a 不乐观
- ☐ b 急脾气
- ☐ c 不自信

阿曼达：王玉，今天还有什么人来？

王玉：还有我的一个好朋友。你们可以认识一下。我觉得你会喜欢她的。

马克：太好了！她叫什么名字？

王玉：她叫凯特，是加拿大人。上个星期刚开始在北京工作。

阿曼达：你们是怎么认识的？

王玉：凯特去年来北京学中文的时候，我是她的老师。

马克：她长什么样子？

王玉：她中等身材，有双蓝色的大眼睛，金色的长卷发，跟我一样高。

阿曼达：是个美女啊！我们应该把她介绍给史蒂夫、永民他们。对了，她的性格怎么样？

王玉：她跟你很像——很乐观、很自信。虽然脾气有一点儿急，但是很关心朋友。凯特喜欢交朋友，喜欢唱歌、跳舞。流行

歌曲和民歌她都会唱，特别是中国民歌《半个月亮爬上来》唱得特别好听。

马克：让我猜一猜，她是不是白羊座的？

王玉：你怎么知道？

马克：我喜欢研究星座，她的性格跟白羊座的很像。

王玉：等她来了，你可以问问她。希望你猜对了。

阿曼达：史蒂夫是狮子座的，听说白羊座跟狮子座很配。

王玉：那一定要把凯特介绍给史蒂夫认识。对了，你们知道中国的属相吗？很多人相信属相跟性格也有关系。

凯特：对不起，我来迟了。

New words

qùnián	去年	last year
juǎnfà	卷发	curly hair
xìnggé	性格	personality
lèguān	乐观	optimistic
zìxìn	自信	self-confident
píqi	脾气	temper, disposition
jí	急	irritable
guānxīn	关心	caring
liúxíng	流行	be popular
gēqǔ	歌曲	song
míngē	民歌	folk song
yuèliang	月亮	moon
cāi	猜	guess
báiyángzuò	白羊座	Aries
yánjiū	研究	research, study
xīngzuò	星座	constellation, star sign
shīzizuò	狮子座	Leo
pèi	配	match
shǔxiang	属相	Chinese zodiac
xiāngxìn	相信	believe
guānxì	关系	relationship, connection

97

3 **Listen again and answer the questions.**

1 凯特的性格怎么样？

2 凯特喜欢做什么？

3 王玉说要把凯特介绍给谁？

4 **Work in pairs. Try to match the personalities with the Chinese zodiac signs.**

a 

b 

c 

d 

1 自信　2 乐观　3 关心人　4 急脾气

5 **Work in groups of four. Discuss who in the class has the characteristics in Activity 4.**

Pronunciation and speaking

Difference between "s" and "sh"

98

1 Check the correct initials for the underlined characters.

1 什么 ☐ s ☐ sh
2 认识 ☐ s ☐ sh
3 森林 ☐ s ☐ sh
4 开始 ☐ s ☐ sh
5 老师 ☐ s ☐ sh
6 蓝色 ☐ s ☐ sh

Now listen and repeat.

99

2 Check the correct pinyin for the words.

1 身材 ☐ sēncái ☐ shēncái
2 时候 ☐ síhou ☐ shíhou
3 金色 ☐ jīnsè ☐ jīnshè
4 虽然 ☐ suīrán ☐ shuīrán
5 狮子 ☐ sīzi ☐ shīzi
6 属相 ☐ sǔxiang ☐ shǔxiang

Now listen and repeat.

100

3 Say the sentences aloud.

Wǒ shì zài Shíshī Shì de shíhou rènshi tā de
1 我是在石狮市的时候认识她的。

Shǐdìfū xǐhuan de diànshìjù shí diǎn kāishǐ
2 史蒂夫 喜欢 的电视剧十 点 开始。

Sì shì sì shí shì shí shísì shì shísì
3 四是四，十是十，十四是十四，
sìshí shì sìshí
四十是四十。

Now listen and repeat.

101

4 Listen and say the words.

1	yàngzi 样子	shēncái 身材	yǎnjing 眼睛	juǎnfà 卷发
2	xìnggé 性格	píqi 脾气	lèguān 乐观	zìxìn 自信
3	xīngzuò 星座	shǔxiang 属相	guānxīn 关心	liúxíng 流行

5 Work in pairs. Ask and answer the questions.

问题	Yes	No
你唱歌唱得好听吗？		
你长得漂亮/帅吗？		
你走路走得快吗？		
你知道朋友的生日吗？		
你有宠物吗？		
你喜欢红色吗？		

Now decide which word best describes your partner's personality.

☐ 自信 ☐ 关心人 ☐ 急脾气

CHINESE TO GO

102

Expressions to describe personality

Tā bú shànyú jiāojì
她（不）善于 交际。 She is (not) good at socialising.

Tā bù hǎo xiāngchǔ
他（不）好 相处。 He is (not) easy to get along with.

Tā de rénpǐn hěn hǎo
她的人品很好。 She has a nice personality.

Nàge rén hěn chīxiāng / xiǎoxīnyǎnr zhíxīnyǎnr
那个人很吃香 / 小心眼儿/直心眼儿。 That person is very popular/ narrow-minded/ straightforward.

báimǎ wángzǐ
白马 王子 Prince Charming

LESSON 2

Reading and writing

1 Work in pairs. Discuss and agree on the three most important characteristics of a good friend, using the words below.

cōngmíng 聪明	clever	zìxìn 自信	self-confident
chéngshí 诚实	honest	lèguān 乐观	optimistic
yǒnggǎn 勇敢	brave	dúlì 独立	independent

103

2 Read and complete the quiz.

New words

hèsè 褐色	brown	chǒngwù 宠物	pet
huīsè 灰色	grey	māo 猫	cat
zhíjiē 直接	direct	gǒu 狗	dog
yìjiàn 意见	opinion	shíjì 实际	practical
bùtóng 不同	different	xiǎoxīn 小心	careful
shāngdiàn 商店	shop	xíngdòng 行动	act, action
dǎgōng 打工	do a temporary job	zǒngshì 总是	always
zhèngqián 挣钱	make money	kǎolǜ 考虑	consider
mǎshàng 马上	immediately, at once	dúlì 独立	independent
zīliào 资料	data, material	cìjī 刺激	exciting
yǎng 养	raise, keep		

Who am I ?

1 我最喜欢的颜色是

a 红色或者黄色。

b 褐色或者灰色。

c 蓝色或者绿色。

2 购物的时候，我会

a 直接去买想要的东西。

b 问朋友的意见。

c 去很多不同的商店，比较东西和价钱。

3 放暑假的时候，我会

a 去打工挣钱。

b 和朋友们一起去旅行、爬山或者潜水。

c 在家里看书或者听音乐。

4 生病的时候，我会

a 马上看医生。

b 打电话给我妈妈，问问应该怎么做。

c 上网查资料。

5 我最想养的宠物是

a 一只猫。

b 一只狗。

c 一条鱼。

10—16	18—22	24—30
你很实际，又很小心。你行动前总是会好好考虑。	你很喜欢交朋友，对朋友很关心，不太独立。	你很独立、自信和乐观，喜欢刺激的生活。

1 a 6 b 2 c 4　2 a 6 b 4 c 2　3 a 2 b 6 c 4　4 a 2 b 4 c 6　5 a 4 b 6 c 2

3 Read again and answer the questions.

1 喜欢刺激生活的人可能会喜欢什么颜色?
2 喜欢交朋友的人可能会养什么宠物?
3 你是什么性格的人?

4 Choose a person in the class and guess what Chinese zodiac sign they might have. Write a description of their characteristics and hobbies, and explain the reasons for your guess.

Now work with the whole class. Find out whether your guesses are correct.

Language in use

Wh-questions

1 Look at the sentences.

Question type				
What	她		叫	什么名字?
	她		叫	凯特。
Who	她		是	谁?
	她		是	我姐姐。
	谁		会来?	
	永民		会来。	
Where	你		住	在哪里?
	我		住	在北京。
When	你	什么时候	去	我家?
	我	周末	去	你家。
Why	马克	为什么	不能来?	
	马克	病了,	不能来。	
How	你们	怎么	去	西安?
	我们	坐火车	去	西安。

Now check the two correct explanations.

☐ 1 The position of question words in Chinese sentences is usually the same as in English.

☐ 2 The position of question words in Chinese sentences is usually different from English.

☐ 3 In replies in Chinese, the answering information usually appears where the question words were.

2 Answer the questions.

1 周末你喜欢做什么?
2 你最喜欢的明星是谁?
3 你喜欢去哪里旅行? 为什么?
4 你什么时候放暑假?
5 你怎样认识新朋友?

Difference between 有（一）点儿 and （一）点儿

1 Look at the sentences.

Subject	Predicate	
	Adverb	Adjective
她的脾气	有（一）点儿	急。
火车	有（一）点儿	不方便。
这个菜	有（一）点儿	辣。

Subject	Predicate		
	Verb	Adjective	Complement
丽莎	需要	独立	（一）点儿。
他	应该	自信	（一）点儿。
你	说	慢	（一）点儿。

Now check the two correct explanations.

☐ 1 有（一）点儿 is often used before an adjective to indicate a positive tone.

☐ 2 （一）点儿 is used after an adjective to indicate the need for more of something.

☐ 3 有（一）点儿 is used before an adjective, while （一）点儿 is used after an adjective.

2 Write the sentences in Chinese.

1 The winter in xi'an is a little cold.
2 You should get up earlier.
3 This dress is a bit too expensive.
4 Could you speak a bit louder?

The auxiliary words 的/地/得

1 Look at the sentences.

Subject	Predicate
永民拍的照片	很漂亮。
凯特	有双蓝色的大眼睛。
他	慢慢地放下了书。
大家	都想快乐地生活。
她	高兴得跳了起来。
王玉	打网球打得很好。

Now check the two correct explanations.

☐ 1 的 is used with an adjective phrase to modify a noun.

☐ 2 地 is used between an adverb or adjective and a verb to describe the purpose of an action.

☐ 3 得 is used between an adjective or a verb and its complement to indicate the result or degree.

2 Complete the sentences with 的, 地 or 得.

1 他跳舞跳 ___ 很好。
2 小明开心 ___ 跳了起来。
3 我很喜欢王玉买 ___ 新裙子。
4 马克在公园拍 ___ 照片很漂亮。
5 她小心 ___ 把电脑放在桌子上面。

Turn to page 170 for grammar reference.

LESSON 3

Communication activity

1 Work in groups of four.

A: You are a matchmaker, trying to find the ideal partner for your client. Create a profile for your client, including their name, appearance, personality, background and Chinese zodiac sign. Draw a picture of your client.

B, C and D: You will each play a suitor for A's client. Create a profile of your character, including background, appearance, personality and hobbies. Be creative!

2 Play the matchmaking game.

A: Introduce your client to the suitors.

B, C and D: As your character, introduce yourself to the matchmaker, emphasising your good points.

A: Ask the suitors questions to find out more about them, and decide which suitor is the best match for your client.

Turn to pages 152 and 158 for more speaking practice.

Cultural corner

The Confucian personality

Confucius (孔子, 551–479BC) was a philosopher who lived during the Spring and Autumn Period (770–467BC) of china. His teachings were required reading for imperial officials from the Han Dynasty onwards. Confucian beliefs have been admired and followed for a long time in China. Even today you can still see elements of Confucian beliefs in Chinese people's perception of personality.

Ren (仁) and *li* (礼) are two important concepts in Confucian thought.

Ren, sometimes translated as "humaneness" or "benevolence", is the inward expression of the Confucian ideal. Confucius described this personality trait as love for others and an understanding of how important your relationships with other people are.

Li literally means "ritual", and in Confucianism means correct behaviour in society. Confucius taught that following *li* in all social relationships would lead to a harmonious society, with everyone knowing their place and showing one another the appropriate respect. So a father should show kindness to his son, and the son should be obedient; a ruler should be benevolent and his subjects loyal; elders should be considerate of their juniors, and the young should defer to them; a husband should be loving and a wife attentive.

Confucius taught that in order to truly follow *li*, one must not only behave outwardly in the proper fashion but also cultivate *ren* within oneself, so the right behaviour will come naturally.

Character writing

These are two common radicals in Chinese. Do you know any other characters with the same radicals?

Radical	Meaning	Example
忄	heart	忙、快
马	horse	马、闯

1 Look at the characters and identify the radicals.

骑　验　怕　慢

2 Match the words with the meanings.

1 测验　　a be afraid
2 性格　　b ride a bike
3 怕　　c quiz
4 骑车　　d personality

3 Trace the characters in the boxes.

性
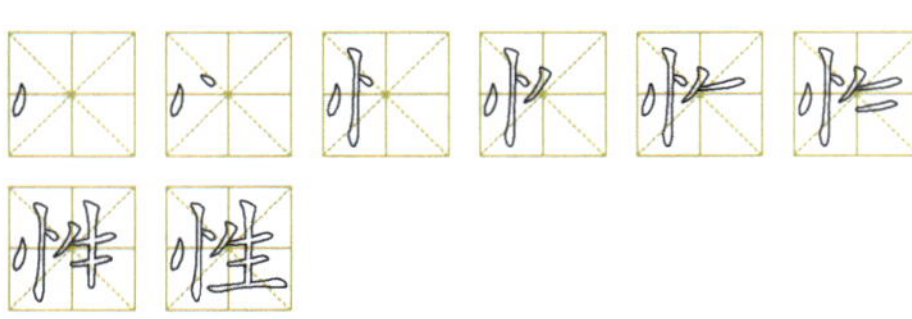

怕
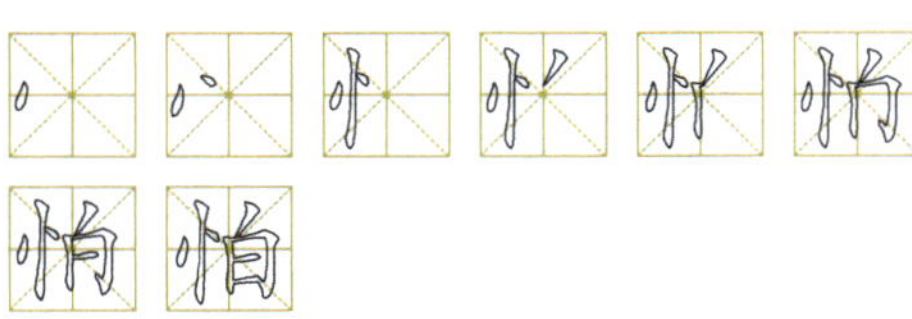

验

骑
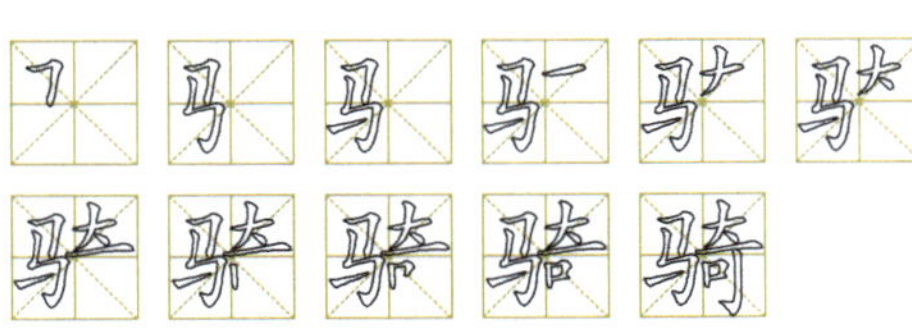

Review and practice

1 Match the words with the meanings.

1 乐观　　a independent
2 自信　　b clever
3 实际　　c optimistic
4 独立　　d practical
5 聪明　　e self-confident

2 Complete the sentences with 有(一)点儿 or (一)点儿.

1 他应该独立 ________。
2 今天天气 ________ 热。
3 白羊座的人脾气 ________ 急。
4 你能不能快 ________？

3 Work in pairs. Ask and answer five wh-questions about each other, using 谁, 什么, 哪里, 什么时候 and 为什么.

4 Work in pairs. Tell each other about your hobbies using 得.

Now tell each other how you do certain things using 地.

5 Imagine you are stranded on a desert island. Write a description of the type of person you would prefer to be with.

Now work in pairs. Ask and answer questions about your partner's description.

Vocabulary extension

1 **Look at the words for personality and check the words that can be used to describe the man on the right.**

nàixīn 耐心	patient	xiūqiè 羞怯	shy
rènzhēn 认真	serious	gùzhi 固执	stubborn
dàfang 大方	generous	bēiguān 悲观	pessimistic

2 **Work in pairs. Talk about two people you both know. Try to use the words above.**

Vocabulary review

Fill in the blanks.

白羊座	báiyángzuò	*n.*	Aries
_____	bùtóng	*adj.*	different
猜	cāi	*v.*	_____
刺激	cìjī	*v.*	exciting
宠物	chǒngwù	*n.*	_____
_____	dǎgōng	*v.*	do a temporary job
独立	dúlì	*adj.*	_____
歌曲	gēqǔ	*n.*	song
_____	gǒu	*n.*	dog
关系	guānxì	*n.*	relationship, connection
_____	guānxīn	*v.*	caring
褐色	hèsè	*n.*	_____
灰色	huīsè	*n.*	_____
_____	jí	*adj.*	irritable
卷发	juǎnfà	*n.*	curly hair
考虑	kǎolǜ	*v.*	_____
乐观	lèguān	*adj.*	_____
流行	liúxíng	*v.*	be popular
_____	mǎshàng	*adv.*	immediately, at once
_____	māo	*n.*	cat
民歌	míngē	*n.*	folk song
配	pèi	*v.*	match
脾气	píqi	*n.*	_____
_____	qùnián	*n.*	last year
_____	shāngdiàn	*n.*	shop
狮子座	shīzizuò	*n.*	_____
实际	shíjì	*adj.*	practical
属相	shǔxiang	*n.*	Chinese zodiac
相信	xiāngxìn	*v.*	_____
_____	xiǎoxīn	*adj.*	careful
星座	xīngzuò	*n.*	constellation, star sign
行动	xíngdòng	*v./n.*	act, action
_____	xìnggé	*n.*	personality
研究	yánjiū	*v.*	research, study
_____	yǎng	*v.*	raise, keep
意见	yìjiàn	*n.*	_____
_____	yuèliang	*n.*	moon
挣钱	zhèngqián	*v.*	_____
直接	zhíjiē	*adj.*	direct
资料	zīliào	*n.*	_____
_____	zìxìn	*adj.*	self-confident
总是	zǒngshì	*adv.*	always
悲观	bēiguān	*adj.*	pessimistic
诚实	chéngshí	*adj.*	honest
聪明	cōngming	*adj.*	clever
大方	dàfang	*adj.*	generous
固执	gùzhi	*adj.*	stubborn
耐心	nàixīn	*adj.*	patient
认真	rènzhēn	*adj.*	serious
羞怯	xiūqiè	*adj.*	shy
勇敢	yǒnggǎn	*adj.*	brave

Review 3

Vocabulary

1 Match the adjectives with the nouns.

1 短	a 脾气
2 矮	b 身材
3 急	c 头发
4 苗条	d 性格
5 乐观	e 个子

2 Circle the odd word out in each line.

1 动物	保护	植物	自然
2 流行	刺激	打工	经常
3 头痛	发烧	身体	着凉
4 眼镜	头发	眼睛	个子
5 湖泊	瀑布	森林	图画

3 Match the verbs with the nouns to make phrases.

1 打	a 朋友
2 吃	b 病
3 检查	c 针
4 治	d 身体
5 关心	e 药

Now write five sentences using the phrases above.

4 Put the words in the correct categories.

a 胖	b 拉肚子	c 雪山
d 发烧	e 卷发	f 树木
g 山水	h 头痛	i 瘦

风景	生病	外表/样子

Grammar

1 Complete the sentences with the correct words.

1 我的作业 ______ 做完了。

a 已经　　b 还没

2 我比我妹妹胖 ______。

a 有一点儿　　b 一点儿

3 明天 ______ 下雪吗？

a 该　　b 会

4 我不发烧了，______ 感觉也好多了。

a 而且　　b 虽然

5 我 ______ 我的手套了。

a 找　　b 找到

2 **Put the words in the correct order to make sentences.**

1 九寨沟/我们/了/到/马上/就要/。

2 我奶奶/上海/看/会/去/暑假/我/。

3 吃饭/和永民/正在/马克/呢/。

4 里/围巾/那条/放在/把/衣柜/。

5 吃/不能/所以/怕/我/辣/川菜/，/。

6 他/一样/瘦/他爸爸/跟/。

3 **Complete the sentences with the words in the box.**

地	的	得	不	没

1 我不太喜欢吃甜 ______。

2 王玉说英语说 ______ 很好。

3 她开心 ______ 跳了起来。

4 他跑 ______ 很快。

5 这里五彩 ______ 湖水真美！

6 每个人都想健康 ______ 生活。

7 你想 ______ 想去听音乐会？

8 永民买 ______ 买那件唐装？

9 你有 ______ 有吃过午饭？

10 这个假期你回 ______ 回家？

4 **Make sentences using the given words.**

1 看电视时间/百分之……

2 除了……以外，还……

3 去美国/看朋友

4 参加除夕派对/庆祝新年

5 今天下午/就要……了

6 明年/就要……了

7 多/吃健康的饭菜

8 少/玩电子游戏

9 跑步/半个小时

Integrated skills

104

1 **Listen and choose the most appropriate responses.**

1 a 没问题。 b 没错儿。

2 a 不错。 b 可以。

3 a 有，我去旅行了。

b 有，我在这里住了两年。

4 a 听不到，你在说话吗？

b 听不到，你可以大声一点儿吗？

5 a 她又高又瘦。

b 她很乐观，也很自信。

6 a 你应该多喝水，好好休息。

b 你应该去跑步，好好吃饭。

2 Complete the sentences with the words in brackets.

1 我觉得肚子不舒服，

______________________。（可能）

2 我在派对上玩得很开心，

______________________。（而且）

3 如果你去成都旅游，

______________________。（一定）

4 凯特很关心朋友，

______________________。（经常）

5 要想病早一点儿好，

______________________。（按时）

3 Work in pairs. Complete the conversation.

王玉：这几天我怎么没有看到你？

马克：______________________。

王玉：你为什么会生病？

马克：______________________。

王玉：你去看医生了吗？

马克：______________________。

王玉：医生给你开药了吗？

马克：______________________。

王玉：希望你很快好起来。

4 Write three sentences to describe each of the following items.

1 我的好朋友（样子，身材，性格）

____

2 我的学校（在哪里，有多大，女学生占百分之几）

____

3 我家附近的公园（多大，有什么，风景特点）

____

Enjoy Chinese

马

马	horse
马车	horse-drawn cart or carriage
骑马	ride a horse
兵马俑	Terracotta Warriors and Horses
马上	immediately, at once

In its ancient form, the character 马 looks like a standing horse. It has a head, four feet, and a tail. As time went on, the character was simplified into its current form. Some Chinese characters are formed by putting different characters together. Can you guess the meaning of the character 闯?

Pair work activities for Student A

Unit 1

1 **You are planning to meet Student B tomorrow to return some books you borrowed. Look at your timetable for tomorrow below.**

时间	要做的事
8:00—10:00	中文课
10:10—11:00	中文考试
11:00—12:00	____________
12:00—13:00	吃午饭
13:00—14:00	去图书馆看书
14:00—16:00	____________
16:00—17:00	踢足球
17:00—18:00	____________
18:00—20:00	跟朋友看电影

2 **Discuss and agree on a good time for you to meet.**

Unit 2

1 **Describe the scene shown in the picture below, including the sorts of clothes you could wear in this kind of weather and the activities you could do.**

2 **Look at the three pictures below. Listen to Student B's description and say which picture is being described.**

a

b

c

Unit 3

1 **Label Plan A with the different rooms and features of your ideal home.**

Plan A

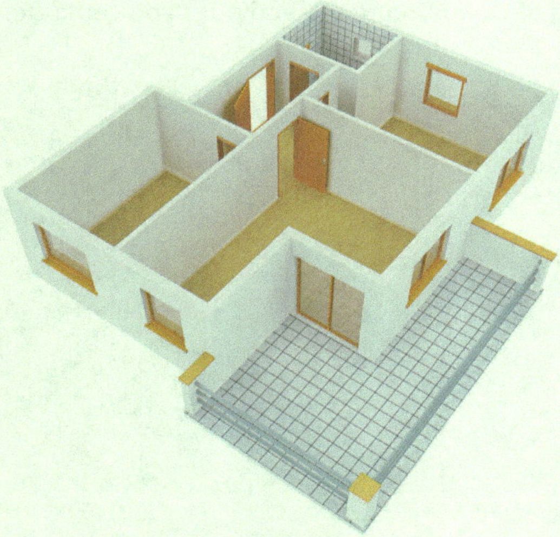

2 **Answer Student B's questions about your ideal home.**

3 **Ask Student B questions and label Plan B with the rooms and features of their dream home.**

Plan B

4 **Compare your plans to find out whose Plan B contains the most accurate details.**

Unit 4

1 **Mark the following places on Map A.**

医院　　邮局　　火车站　　出租车站

Map A

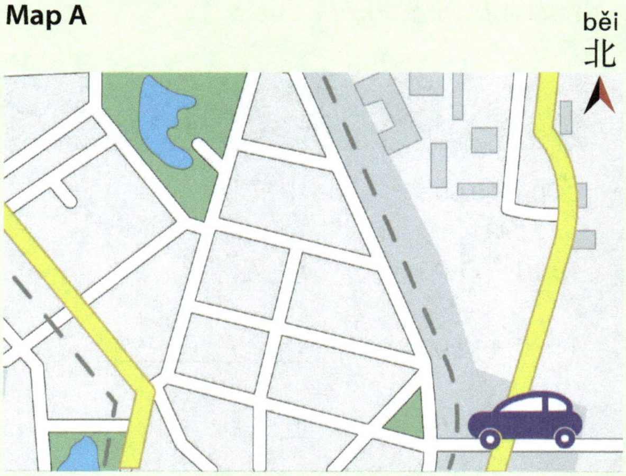

2 **Answer Student B's questions about how to get to the places you marked on Map A.**

3 **Ask Student B questions about how to get to the following places and mark them on Map B.**

宾馆　银行　博物馆　地铁站

Map B

4 **Compare your maps to find out whose Map B contains the most accurate details.**

Unit 5

1 Look carefully at the picture. You have one minute to memorise as many details as possible.

2 Close your book. Describe the picture from memory, using 旁边, 对面, 上面, 下面 when necessary.

3 Listen to Student B describing a room, and draw it.

4 Compare your drawings with the original pictures to find out whose drawing contains the most accurate details.

Unit 6

1 Mime the following signs to Student B.

2 Guess what Student B is miming, in Chinese.

Unit 7

1 **Look at the ingredients and choose three to make a dish. Add two ingredients of your choice.**

zhūròu 猪肉	yángròu 羊肉	niúròu 牛肉	jīròu 鸡肉
yúròu 鱼肉	jīdàn 鸡蛋	mǐfàn 米饭	Yìdàlìmiàn 意大利面

2 **Write a recipe for your dish, including the ingredients and the cooking steps.**

3 **Explain to Student B how to make your dish, without saying its name.**

4 **Listen and guess the name of the dish that Student B is describing.**

Unit 8

1 **Choose three souvenirs of a trip to China from the objects below—two as gifts for friends and one to keep for yourself.**

2 **Ask Student B about the colour, size and use of the souvenirs they have chosen. Guess what they are (don't ask what they are).**

3 **Answer Student B's questions about your souvenirs (don't say what they are).**

Unit 9

1 Describe the scenery in the picture.

2 Listen to Student B's description of their picture.

3 Ask each other questions to find out the differences between your pictures.

Unit 10

1 Describe the appearance of the girl in the picture.

2 Listen to Student B's description of the girl in the picture when she is 30 years old.

3 Ask each other questions to find out how her appearance has changed.

Unit 11

1 You have a headache, a blocked nose and a cough, and you want to buy some medicine at a pharmacy. Prepare some questions to ask the pharmacist about the medicine they give you. Use the words below.

yàomíng 药名	medicine name
bùliáng fǎnyìng 不良 反应	side effects

2 Answer Student B's questions about your symptoms.

3 Ask Student B questions about the details of the medicine.

Unit 12

1 Describe the two candidates who are applying for the post of Student Events Manager at your school.

姓名: Jessica
国籍: 巴西
性格: 自信、乐观
爱好: 跳舞、潜水

姓名: Jean-Philippe
国籍: 法国
性格: 独立、自信
爱好: 唱民歌、购物

2 Listen to Student B's description of two candidates.

3 Ask each other questions about the candidates. Choose the best person for the job from the four candidates.

Pair work activities for Student B

Unit 1

1 You are planning to meet Student A tomorrow to get some books. Look at your timetable for tomorrow below.

时间	要做的事
8:00—10:00	英文课
10:10—11:00	____________
11:00—12:00	复习准备考试
12:00—13:00	____________
13:00—14:00	跟朋友们一起吃午饭
14:00—16:00	____________
16:00—17:00	去超市买东西
17:00—18:00	做作业
18:00—20:00	____________

2 Discuss and agree on a good time for you to meet.

Unit 2

1 Look at the three pictures below. Listen to Student A's description and say which of the three is being described.

a

b

c

2 Describe the scene shown in the picture below, including the sorts of clothes you could wear in this kind of weather and the activities you could do.

Unit 3

1 Label Plan A with the different rooms and features of your ideal home.

Plan A

2 Ask Student A questions and label Plan B with the rooms and features of their dream home.

Plan B

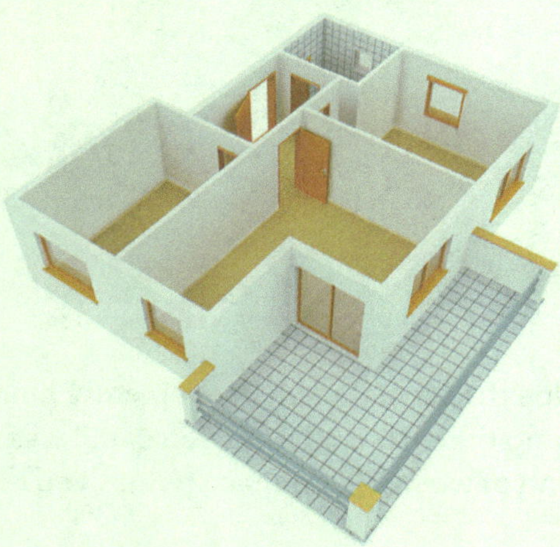

3 Answer Student A's questions about your ideal home.

4 Compare your plans to find out whose Plan B contains the most accurate details.

Unit 4

1 Mark these places on Map A.

宾馆　银行　博物馆　地铁站

Map A

2 Ask Student A questions about how to get to the following places and mark them on Map B.

医院　邮局　火车站　出租车站

Map B

3 Answer Student A's questions about how to get to the places you marked on Map A.

4 Compare your maps to find out whose Map B contains the most accurate details.

Unit 5

1 Listen to Student A describing a room, and draw it.

2 Look carefully at the picture. You have one minute to memorise as many details as possible.

3 Close your book. Describe the picture from memory, using 旁边, 对面, 上面, 下面 when necessary.

4 Compare your drawings with the original pictures to find out whose drawing contains the most accurate details.

Unit 6

1 Guess what Student A is miming, in Chinese.

2 Mime the following signs to Student A.

Unit 7

1 Look at the ingredients and choose three to make a dish. Add two ingredients of your choice.

zhūròu 猪肉	yángròu 羊肉	niúròu 牛肉	jīròu 鸡肉
yúròu 鱼肉	jīdàn 鸡蛋	mǐfàn 米饭	Yìdàlìmiàn 意大利面

2 Write a recipe for your dish, including the ingredients and the cooking steps.

3 Listen and guess the name of the dish that Student A is describing.

4 Explain to Student A how to make your dish, without saying its name.

Unit 8

1 Choose three souvenirs of a trip to China from the objects below—two as gifts for friends and one to keep for yourself.

2 Answer Student A's questions about your souvenirs (do not say what they are).

3 Ask Student A about the colour, size, and use of the souvenirs they have chosen. Guess what they are (do not ask what they are).

Unit 9

1. Listen to Student A's description of their picture.
2. Describe the scenery in the picture.

3. Ask each other questions to find out the differences between your pictures.

Unit 10

1. Listen to Student A's description of the woman in the picture below when she was seven years old.
2. Describe the appearance of the woman in the picture.

3. Ask each other questions to find out how her appearance has changed.

Unit 11

1 You are a pharmacist. Read the medicine label and prepare to answer questions about it.

yàomíng 药名 ：	Gǎnmàoqīng 感冒 清
zhǔzhì 主治：	gǎnmào fāshāo bísè 感冒 ， 发烧， 鼻塞
bùliáng fǎnyìng 不良 反应：	kǒu gān wèibù bù shūfu 口 干、胃部 不 舒服、 wúlì tóuyūn děng 无力、头晕 等
yòngfǎ yòngliàng 用法 用量 ：	kǒufú měi bā xiǎoshí fú 口服， 每 8 小时 服 sān piàn dào sì piàn èrshísì 3 片 到 4 片， 24 xiǎoshí nèi bù néng duō yú 小时 内 不 能 多 于 shí' èr piàn 12 片
zhùyì shìxiàng 注意 事项 ：	fú yào shí bù néng hē jiǔ 服 药 时 不 能 喝 酒

2 Ask Student A questions about their symptoms.

3 Answer Student A's questions about the medicine.

Unit 12

1 Listen to Student A's description of two candidates who are applying for the post of Student Events Manager at your school.

2 Describe these two candidates who are applying for the same post.

姓名：Pak Jimin
国籍：韩国
性格：关心别人、诚实
爱好：在家看书、听音乐

姓名：Stefan
国籍：德国
性格：急脾气、勇敢
爱好：蹦极、滑雪

3 Ask each other questions about the candidates. Choose the best person for the job from the four candidates.

Grammar reference

Unit 1

The auxiliary word 得 (de)

The auxiliary word 得 is used between a verb and its complement to indicate result or degree. An adjective phrase is used after 得 as the verb complement. There can be two verbs in a sentence with 得 to indicate the complement. The first verb phrase describes an event, while the second verb describes the exact action involved in the event. The second verb should be the same as the verb included in the first verb phrase. To negate the sentence, the adverb 不 is used at the beginning of the adjective phrase as part of the complement. For example,

Subject	Verb phrase	Verb	得 (de)	Complement
Mǎkè 马克		tiào 跳	de 得	hěn gāo 很高。
Mark jumps very high.				
Tā 他		pǎo 跑	de 得	kuài 快。
He runs quickly.				
Nǐ 你	chànggē 唱歌	chàng 唱	de 得	hěn hǎotīng 很好听。
You sing very well.				
Tā 她	tiàowǔ 跳舞	tiào 跳	de 得	bù hǎo 不好。
She does not dance well.				
Mèimei 妹妹	chīfàn 吃饭	chī 吃	de 得	hěn màn 很慢。
My little sister eats very slowly.				
Wǒ 我	kàn shū 看书	kàn 看	de 得	bú kuài 不快。
I don't read books very quickly.				

Topic-comment sentences

When a piece of information is already known to the speakers, it is often put at the beginning of a sentence as the subject. This structure is called a topic-comment sentence, which is different from the usual word order of Chinese sentences.

For example,

Topic	Comment
Xīngqīsān de kǎoshì 星期三的考试	wǒ zhǔnbèi hǎo le 我准备好了。
I have finished preparing for Wednesday's test.	
Xīngqītiān yìqǐ qù chīfàn 星期天一起去吃饭	tā hái bù zhīdào 她还不知道。
She still doesn't know about going to eat together on Sunday.	
Míngtiān jiāo zuòyè 明天交作业	dāngrán bù kěnéng 当然不可能。
Of course it's impossible to hand in the homework tomorrow.	
Yìbiān gōngzuò yìbiān dúshū 一边工作一边读书	tài nán le 太难了。
Working and studying at the same time is too difficult.	

了 (le) as a particle and an auxiliary word

Besides being used as an auxiliary word placed after a verb to indicate that an action has taken place, 了 can also be used as a particle placed at the end of a sentence to indicate a statement, showing a change of situation or state. For example,

Subject	Predicate
Tā 他	qù le Běijīng 去了北京。
He has gone to Beijing.	
Nǐ 你	chīfàn le ma 吃饭了吗?
Have you eaten?	
Wǒ 我	zhīdào zhè jiàn shì le 知道这件事了。
I know (now) about this whole thing.	
Wáng Yù 王玉	qù shàngkè le 去上课了。
Wang Yu has gone to class.	

Indicating succession using 一(yī)……就(jiù)……

一……就…… is used to connect two events or actions that happen one right after the other. It means "as soon as". The subjects of the two actions or events can be the same or different.

For example,

Wǒ yí dào Xī'ān jiù gěi nǐ dǎ diànhuà
我一到西安，就给你打电话。

As soon as I reach Xi'an, I'll give you a call.

Wǒ yì huílai tā jiù chūqù
我一回来，他就出去。

As soon as I came back, he went out.

一……就…… can also be used to connect a time phrase and an action or event, meaning something will happen as soon as the time comes. For example,

Yí dào zhōumò tā jiù qù kàn yéye
一到周末，她就去看爷爷。

As soon as the weekend comes, she'll go to see her grandpa.

Yí dào shǔjià wǒ jiù qù lǚxíng
一到暑假，我就去旅行。

Once it's the summer holidays, I'm going to travel.

Yí dào wǎnshang jiǔ diǎn wǒ jiù shàng chuáng shuìjiào
一到晚上九点，我就上床睡觉。

When it is 9 o'clock, I'll go to bed.

Unit 2

hé chàbuduō yíyàng

Describing similarity using A和B + 差不多/ 一样

A和B + **差不多/一样** is used to describe similarity between two things. **差不多** is often used alone as the predicate, meaning "about the same". **一样** means "the same" or "identical". It can stand alone, or be followed by an adjective as its complement stating the specific details of the similarity. For example,

A	hé 和	B	Adjective	Complement
Zhè jiàn yīfu 这件衣服 de jiàqián 的价钱	hé 和	nà jiàn 那件 yīfu de （衣服的 jiàqián 价钱）	chàbuduō 差不多。	
The prices of this item of clothing and that one are about the same.				
Běijīng de 北京的 tiānqì 天气	hé 和	Niǔyuē de 纽约的 tiānqì （天气）	chàbuduō 差不多 ma 吗?	
Is the weather in Beijing and New York similar?				
Zhèli de 这里的 qìwen 气温	hé 和	nàli de 那里的 qìwen （气温）	yíyàng 一样。	
The temperature here is the same as there.				
Mèimei 妹妹	hé 和	jiějie 姐姐	yíyàng 一样	piàoliang 漂亮。
The younger and elder sisters are equally pretty.				

bǐ méiyǒu

Making comparisons using A 比/没有B + adjective

A比B + adjective is used to make a comparison between two things, meaning the former is higher in degree than the latter. **没有** is used to indicate that A is less or lower in degree than B. When the same head noun is used in both A and B, the head noun in B can be left out to avoid repetition. For example,

A	bǐ méiyǒu 比/没有	B	Adjective
Zhōngguó 中国 dàxué de 大学的 shàngkè shíjiān 上课 时间	bǐ 比	Yīngguó dàxué 英国大学 de shàngkè 的（上课 shíjiān 时间）	zǎo 早。
Classes in Chinese universities start earlier than those in British universities.			
Jīntiān de tiānqì 今天的天气	bǐ 比	zuótiān de 昨天的 tiānqì （天气）	hǎo 好。
Today's weather is nicer than yesterday's.			
Zhèxiē zhàopiàn 这些 照片	méiyǒu 没有	nàxiē 那些 zhàopiàn （照片）	piàoliang 漂亮。
These photographs are not as pretty as those.			
Xī'ān 西安	méiyǒu 没有	Běijīng 北京	dà 大。
Xi'an is not as big as Beijing.			

Describing future actions with 要/会 (yào huì)

要 can be a modal verb, meaning 需要 (need). For example, 我要买一件大衣. (I need to buy an overcoat.)

When 要 is used to describe future actions, it usually indicates something that the speaker intends to do. For example, 我要去看电影. (I'm going to see a film.)

Besides indicating ability (e.g. 她会说日语), the modal verb 会 can also be used to describe a future event, indicating a high probability. 不 is used before 会 to negate sentences about future events. Sometimes 的 is used at the end of the sentences to strengthen the certainty.

Adverbial of time	Subject	Modal verb	Verb phrase
Jīntiān wǎnshang 今天 晚上	Yǒngmín 永民	huì 会	lái ma 来吗?
Will Yeong-min come tonight?			
	Tā 他	bú huì 不会	lái le 来了。
He won't come.			
	Wǒ 我	huì 会	gěi nǐ dǎ diànhuà de 给你打电话的。
I'm going to phone you.			
Zhōumò 周末	wǒ 我	huì 会	qù kàn nǐ de 去看你的。
I'm going to see you at the weekend.			

Unit 3

Describing actions in progress using 正在 (zhèngzài)

正在 is an adverb used before a verb phrase to indicate that something is taking place or someone is right in the middle of doing something at the time mentioned. Either 正 or 在 can be left out if the emphasis is on the event as a whole instead of something happening at that moment. Sometimes 呢 can be used at the end of a progressive sentence to emphasise the continuousness of the action or event. For example,

Adverbial	Subject	zhèngzài 正在	Verb phrase	ne 呢
	Wǒ 我	zhèngzài 正在	mǎi dōngxi 买东西。	
I am shopping.				
Zuótiān xiàwǔ 昨天 下午 sì diǎn 四点	Yǒngmín 永民	zhèng (正) zài 在	dǎ lánqiú 打篮球	ne 呢。
At four yesterday afternoon, Yeong-min was playing basketball.				
Nǐ dǎ diànhuà 你打电话 de shíhou 的时候,	wǒ 我	zhèng 正 zài (在)	kàn diànshì 看电视	ne 呢。
I was watching TV when you phoned.				

Expressing "both... and..." with 又……又…… (yòu yòu)

又……又…… is used to describe equal characteristics of a person or entity, and concurrent actions, events or circumstances. It can be used to link verb phrases and adjective phrases. The words connected by 又……又…… should be of the same structure or part of speech, indicating that the things do not contradict each other. When adjective phrases are linked, the adverb 很, meaning "very" and usually being placed before the adjectives, can be left out. For example,

Time/Place/Manner	First condition/quality	Second condition/quality
	Dìtiě hěn kuài 地铁很快。	Dìtiě hěn piányi 地铁很便宜。
Dìtiě yòu kuài yòu piányi 地铁又快又便宜。		
The subway is both fast and cheap.		
Zài pàiduì shang 在派对上,	tā chànggē 他唱歌,	tā tiàowǔ 他跳舞。
Zài pàiduì shang 在派对上,	tā yòu chànggē yòu tiàowǔ 他又唱歌又跳舞。	
At the party, he was singing and dancing.		

Describing sequences with 先……然后……

xiān ránhòu

先……然后…… describes a succession of actions or sequence of events. 先 must be placed after the subject of the first action or event, while 然后 is usually placed before the subject of the following action or event. The second subject is often left out if it is the same as the first subject. For example,

First event/action	Second event/action
Wǒ xiān kàn shū 我 先 看 书，	ránhòu qù dǎ wǎngqiú 然后 去 打 网球 。
First I read, then I go to play tennis.	
Wáng Yù xiān qù kàn 王 玉 先 去 看 yéye 爷爷，	ránhòu hé Shǐdìfū kàn 然后 和史蒂夫 看 diànyǐng 电影 。
First Wang Yu went to see her grandfather, then she watched a film with Steve.	
Míngtiān wǒ yào xiān qù 明天 我 要 先 去 yínháng 银行，	ránhòu qù chāoshì mǎi 然后 去 超市 买 dōngxi 东西。
Tomorrow I'm going to go to the bank first, then I'll go shopping at the supermarket.	

Unit 4

Talking about distance using 离/多远

lí duōyuǎn

离 is used to indicate how far away one place is from the other. The subject takes the form of A离B. The distance can be described simply with an adjective, precisely with physical distance, or approximately with time spent on transportation. For example,

Subject	Predicate
Wǒ jiā lí xuéxiào 我 家 离 学校	hěn jìn 很 近。
My home is very close to the university.	
Xīní lí Mò'ěrběn 悉尼 离 墨尔本	dàyuē gōnglǐ 大约 900 公里。
Sydney is about 900 km from Melbourne.	
Niǔyuē lí Bōshìdùn 纽约 离 波士顿	kāi chē dàyuē sì gè xiǎoshí 开 车 大约 四 个 小时。
New York is about four hours' drive from Boston.	

If the starting or ending point of a distance is obviously known in the context, 离 and the known point can be left out of the sentence. For example,

Nǐ jiā duō yuǎn
你 家 多 远？ How far away is your home?

Zǒulù shí fēnzhōng
走路 十 分钟 。 It takes ten minutes on foot.

Describing distance using 从 A 到 B

cóng dào

从A到B is used to describe the distance between two places, with A being the starting point and B the ending point. The topic takes the form 从A到B, which is often followed by a comment including a verb phrase and the duration of time.

Topic				Comment	
cóng 从	A	dào 到	B	Verb phrase	Duration
Cóng 从	Lúndūn 伦敦	dào 到	Bālí 巴黎，	zuò gāosù 坐 高速 huǒchē 火车	zuì fāngbiàn 最 方便 。
Taking a high-speed train is the most convenient way to go from London to Paris.					
Cóng 从	xuéxiào 学校	dào 到	wǒ jiā 我 家	zǒulù 走路	shí fēnzhōng 十 分钟 。
It takes ten minutes to walk from the university to my house.					
Cóng 从	Xī'ān 西安	dào 到	Běijīng 北京	kāi chē 开车	shíjiān hěn cháng 时间 很 长 。
It takes a very long time to drive from Xi'an to Beijing.					

从A到B can also be used to indicate the starting and ending points of a period of time. For example,

Cóng Xīngqīyī dào Xīngqīwǔ měi tiān wǒ dōu yǒu hěn duō
从 星期一 到 星期五，每 天 我 都 有 很 多
zuòyè
作业。

I have a lot of homework from Monday to Friday.

Cóng xiǎo dào dà wǒ dōu hěn xǐhuan chànggē
从 小 到 大，我 都 很 喜欢 唱歌 。

I have liked singing very much since childhood.

Using 以后/……的 时候

(yǐhòu / de shíhou)

以后 is used together with a verb phrase or time phrase to indicate a sequence of actions or events, meaning "after". It is used at the end of an adverbial phrase or clause denoting time, which can be put before or after the subject of the sentence. For example,

Adverbial clause	Subject	Adverbial	Predicate
Huíjiā yǐhòu 回家以后，	wǒ 我		gěi Ānnà dǎ diànhuà 给安娜打电话。
After I got home, I telephoned Anna.			
Liǎng nián yǐhòu 两 年以后，	Xiǎomíng 小明		yào qù Měiguó 要去美国。
In two years, Xiaoming will go to America.			
	Wǒ māma 我妈妈	sān tiān 三天 yǐhòu 以后	lái kàn wǒ 来看我。
My mother will come to see me in three days.			

……的时候 is also used at the end of an adverbial phrase or clause denoting time, meaning "when".

Adverbial clause	Subject	Predicate
Fàngxué de shíhou 放学 的时候，	Mǎkè 马克	hái méiyǒu zuò wán zuòyè 还没有做完作业。
When class finished, Mark had not finished his homework.		
Chī wǎnfàn de shíhou 吃晚饭的时候，	wǒ 我	qù le diànyǐngyuàn 去了 电影院 。
At dinner time, I went to the cinema.		

Unit 5

Indicating possession, existence or location with 有

(yǒu)

有 is used to indicate possession. The subject of the sentence with 有 can be a person or a thing. For example,

Wǒ yǒu hěn duō gùshi shū
我有很多故事书。 I have a lot of story books.

Xī'ān yǒu jǐ qiān nián de lìshǐ
西安有几千 年的历史。

Xi'an has several thousand years of history.

有 can also be used to indicate the existence or location of one thing in relation to another. The subject is usually a locative phrase, which contains or is equal in size to the object. For example,

Locative phrase		Verb	Noun phrase
Wǒ de yīguì 我的衣柜	li 里	yǒu 有	hěn duō yīfu 很多衣服。
There are a lot of clothes in my wardrobe.			
Zhuōzi 桌子	xiàmiàn 下面	yǒu 有	yì shuāng xié 一双鞋。
There's a pair of shoes under the table.			
Wǒ de gōngyù 我的公寓	qiánmiàn 前面	yǒu 有	yí gè chāoshì 一个超市。
There is a supermarket in front of my flat.			
Xuéxiào 学校	dōngbian 东边	yǒu 有	yí gè diànyǐngyuàn 一个 电影院。
There is a cinema to the east of the university.			

Indicating adequacy with 够/不 够

(gòu bú gòu)

够 is used as a verb with its own complement, meaning "be enough/sufficient" or "reach (a standard)". Its negative form is 不够.

For example,

Wǒmen diǎn de cài gòu ma
我们点的菜够吗？

Have we ordered enough food?

Wǒ de shíjiān bú gòu yòng
我的时间不够用。

I don't have enough time.

够 can also be used as an adverb before some adjectives, meaning "enough" or "really". For example,

Jīntiān de tiānqì gòu lěng wǒmen kěyǐ chī huǒguō
今天的天气够冷，我们可以吃火锅。

Today's weather is cold enough for us to have hot pot.

Kāi chē gòu kuài bàn gè xiǎoshí jiù kěyǐ dào
开车够快，半个小时就可以到

Bīngmǎyǒng bówùguǎn
兵马俑博物馆。

If you drive really fast, it will take only half an hour to get to the Museum of Terracotta Warriors and Horses.

Complements indicating results

An adjective or a verb phrase is often used after a verb as its complement to indicate the result. For example,

Subject	Verb	Complement
Wǒ 我	xiě 写	wán le 完了。
I have finished writing.		
Tā de shǒujī 她的手机	zhǎo 找	bú dào le 不到了。
She couldn't find her mobile phone.		
Nǐ 你	kàn 看	dǒng le ma 懂了吗？
Did you understand that?		
Wǒ 我	zhǔnbèi 准备	hǎo le 好了。
I'm (fully) ready.		
Yīfu 衣服	xǐ 洗	gānjìng le 干净了。
The clothes have been cleaned.		
Nǐ 你	zuò 做	duì le 对了。
You did it right.		

Questions about sizes with (有)多大/长/宽

yǒu duō dà cháng kuān

多 means "to what extent" when used in questions. It is often used to modify words indicating measurements such as 大, 长, 宽, 高 etc. The verb 有 is optionally used in the questions about sizes. In answers to questions about sizes, the words indicating measurements can be used as the predicate. 有 can also be used to introduce the size followed by the word indicating measurement.

Question

Subject	Predicate	
	Verb	Question word
Zhège tǐyùchǎng 这个体育场	yǒu （有）	duō dà 多大？
How big is the stadium?		

Answers

Subject	Verb	Measurement	Size	Measurement
Zhège tǐyùchǎng 这个体育场		cháng 长	mǐ 500 米。	
Zhège tǐyùchǎng 这个体育场	yǒu （有）		mǐ 500 米	cháng 长。
This stadium is 500 metres long.				
Zhège tǐyùchǎng 这个体育场		kuān 宽	mǐ 400 米。	
Zhège tǐyùchǎng 这个体育场	yǒu （有）		mǐ 400 米	kuān 宽。
This stadium is 400 metres wide.				

Unit 6

Indicating passive voice using 被 (bèi)

被 is used to form a passive voice sentence, emphasising the object being acted upon and the change that takes place as a consequence of the action. The object being acted upon is used as the subject before 被. The doer of the action is used after 被, and can be omitted if it is not known or not necessary to be mentioned.

Subject	Adverbial		Verb	Complement
	bèi 被	Doer		
Wǒ de yīfu 我的衣服	bèi 被	rén （人）	ná 拿	zǒu le 走了。
My clothes were taken (by someone).				
Wǒ de wǎnfàn 我的晚饭	bèi 被	dìdi 弟弟	chī 吃	le 了。
My dinner was eaten by my little brother.				
Zhè běn shū 这本书	bèi 被	tā 他	mǎi 买	le 了。
This book was bought by him.				

Indicating a continuing action or state with 着 (zhe)

着 is used after a verb to indicate the continuation of an action or a state. The verb should be stative, indicating the status of something resulting from an action, such as 穿, 戴, 坐, 写, 放, 贴, 挂 etc.

For example,

Subject	Verb	zhe 着	Object
Yǒngmín 永民	dài 戴	zhe 着	tàiyángjìng 太阳镜。
Yeong-min wears sunglasses.			
Tā 她	chuān 穿	zhe 着	hóng qúnzi 红 裙子。
She wears a red skirt.			
Fángjiān li 房间 里	zuò 坐	zhe 着	yí wèi xiānsheng 一位 先生 。
There is a gentleman sitting in the room.			
Zhuōzi shang 桌子 上	fàng 放	zhe 着	yí gè diànhuà 一个 电话。
A telephone is on the table.			
Ménkǒu 门口	guà 挂	zhe 着	hóng dēnglong 红 灯笼 。
Red lanterns hang from the gate.			

是 (shì)……的 (de) constructions

是……的 is used to talk about a certain aspect of a past action or event. In this structure the focus is not on the action or event itself, but on one aspect of the action such as time, place, manner, purpose or target of the action or event.

是 is usually placed right after the subject and can be omitted in an affirmative or interrogative sentence, while 的 is put at the end of the sentence and cannot be omitted.

Subject	shì 是	Time/Place/ Manner	Predicate	de 的
Nǐ 你	shì 是	zěnme 怎么	rènshi tā 认识她	de 的？
How did you know her?				
Wǒ 我	shì 是	zài Běijīng 在北京	rènshi tā 认识她	de 的。
I met her in Beijing.				

Subject	shì 是	Time/Place/ Manner	Predicate	de 的
Nǐ 你	shì （是）	shénme shíhou 什么 时候	qù Měiguó 去 美国	de 的？
When did you go to America?				
Wǒ 我	shì （是）	shàng gè yuè 上 个 月	qù 去	de 的。
I went last month.				

In addition, if the main verb is followed by an object, 的 can be put either before or after the object. For example,

Wǒ shì zuótiān qù de xuéxiào
我 是 昨天 去 的 学校。

Wǒ shì zuótiān qù xuéxiào de
我 是 昨天 去 学校 的。

I went to the university yesterday.

Unit 7

Noun phrases with 的 (de)

的 is used after a noun, pronoun, verb or adjective to form a noun phrase. It is used to refer to someone or something that is already known in the context. Therefore the head noun is usually left out. 的 can also be used to indicate a certain type of people or thing.

Referring to a known object/person	
adjective + 的 (de)	Gōngyuán li de huā kāi le, yǒu hóng de, yǒu huáng de 公园 里 的 花 开 了，有 红 的，有 黄 的。 The flowers in the park have bloomed. There are red and yellow ones.
pronoun + 的 (de)	Zhè bù shǒujī bú shì wǒ de, shì tā de 这 部 手机 不 是 我 的，是 他 的。 This mobile phone isn't mine. It's his.
noun + 的 (de)	Tāmen de yīfu dōu shì hēisè de 他们 的 衣服 都 是 黑色 的。 Their clothes are all black.
verb + 的 (de)	Tā shuō de bú duì 他 说 的 不 对。 What he said is not correct.

Indicating a certain category	
adjective + 的 (de)	Wǒ xǐhuan chī tián de 我喜欢吃甜的。 I like eating sweet things.
noun + 的 (de)	Xīn tóngxué shì gè nán de 新同学是个男的。 The new classmate is male.

Giving instructions using imperatives

Imperatives are commonly used to give instructions, orders or make requests. As the instruction or request is usually directed to the hearer, the subject is understood by both parties, and therefore often dropped. Other than that, an imperative is similar to an ordinary statement. The verb 请 is often used at the beginning of an imperative to make it sound polite, and 吧 is often added at the end of an imperative to soften the tone.

Adverbial	Verb	Object
Zài guō li 在锅里	jiā 加	yì wǎn jītāng 一碗鸡汤。
Add a bowl of chicken soup to the pot.		
Qǐng gěi wǒ 请给我	ná 拿	yì bēi shuǐ 一杯水。
Please bring me a glass of water.		
	Chī 吃	fàn ba 饭吧！
Eat please!		

把 (bǎ) sentences

The 把 construction includes the agent, the object acted on, the action itself and the result of the action. The object is usually a definite noun, known to both the speaker and hearer. The result of the action can be an adjective or noun indicating the changed state of the object, or a place or person that is involved in the action.

Subject	bǎ 把	Object	Verb	Complement
	Bǎ 把	ròu 肉	chǎo 炒	shú 熟。
Stir-fry the meat until cooked.				
	Bǎ 把	cōng 葱	qiē 切	chéng mò 成末。
Finely chop the spring onions.				
Wǒ 我	bǎ 把	Zhōngwén shū 中文书	fàng 放	zài jiā li le 在家里了。
I left the Chinese book at home.				

Unit 8

Duplication of verbs

Duplication of verbs is used to soften the tone of a sentence. By duplicating a verb, the speaker wants to sound either less decisive, or more polite. Duplication of verbs is often used when making suggestions or requests. 一 can be placed between the duplicated verbs to express a mild tone.

Subject	Verb	Object	Other
Wǒ 我	kànkan 看看	nǐ de shū 你的书，	kěyǐ ma 可以吗？
Is it OK for me to have a look at your book?			
Nǐ 你	chángchang 尝尝	wǒ zuò de jiǎozi 我做的饺子。	
Have a taste of the dumplings I made.			
Wǒmen 我们	dǎda 打打	wǎngqiú 网球，	zěnmeyàng 怎么样？
We'll play a bit of tennis, OK?			
Nǐ 你	shì yí shì 试一试	zhè tiáo kùzi 这条裤子。	
Try on this pair of trousers.			

"The more… the more…" 越 (yuè)……越 (yuè)……

越……越…… is used to link a verb or adjective with a verb phrase or adjective phrase, meaning the degree increases as something goes on or increases.

Subject	yuè 越	Verb/ Adjective	yuè 越	Verb phrase/ Adjective phrase
Wǒ 我	yuè 越	chī 吃	yuè 越	xiǎng chī 想 吃。
The more I eat, the more I want to eat.				
Tā 他	yuè 越	shuō 说	yuè 越	bù gāoxìng 不 高兴。
The more he talks, the less happy he is.				
Xiǎomíng 小 明	yuè 越	gāoxìng 高兴	yuè 越	bù xiǎng zǒu 不 想 走。
The happier Xiaomíng was, the less he wanted to leave.				
Wèntí 问题	yuè 越	shǎo 少	yuè 越	hǎo 好。
The fewer problems the better.				

Notional passive

Notional passive is used when the focus is on how the object is dealt with and the result of the action, without the need to mention the doer or agent of the action. In a notional passive sentence, the object being acted upon is used as the subject, followed by a verb and its complement. There is no 被 in a notional passive sentence. A notional passive sentence sounds more active than a passive voice sentence with 被, as the focus is on the result or changed state of the object acted upon. For example,

Biǎo tián wán le
表 填 完 了。

The form is filled in.

Zuòyè fàng zài jiā li le
作业 放 在 家 里 了。

The homework has been left at home.

Shǒutào zhǎo bú dào le
手套 找 不 到 了。

The gloves could not be found.

Unit 9

Indicating the result of an action with 到 (dào)

到 can be used after many different verbs to form a verb complement indicating the result of an action. Depending on the meaning of the verbs, the verb complement can be a place or an object following 到. For instance, when used after 回 or 来, the complement with 到 indicates a place.

Verb	Complement	
	dào 到	Place
huí 回	dào 到	sùshè 宿舍
return to the dormitory		
lái 来	dào 到	xuéxiào 学校
come to the school/university		
lái 来	dào 到	Běijīng 北京
come to Beijing		

When used after sensory verbs (看, 听, 想) or action verbs (找, 拿, 买), the complement with 到 indicates an object. 不 is used between the verb and 到 to indicate a negative result. For example,

Verb	Complement	
	dào 到	Object
kàn 看	dào 到	hěn duō rén 很 多 人
see many people		
zhǎo 找	bú dào （不）到	wǒ mèimei 我 妹妹
(can't) find my little sister		
ná 拿	bú dào （不）到	bàozhǐ 报纸
(can't) pick up a newspaper		
mǎi 买	dào 到	yí jiàn hěn hǎokàn de xù 一 件 很 好看 的 T 恤
bought a very nice-looking T-shirt		

Expressing percentages using 百分之 (bǎifēnzhī)……

占……百分之…… is used to express the percentage of something in a group. 占 means "constitute", "make up" or "account for". An adjective phrase is used before 百分之 to state what a thing is a proportion of. It can be left out if this is known in the context.

For example,

Subject	Verb	Adjective phrase	Percentage
Shuìjiào shíjiān 睡觉 时间	zhàn 占	suǒyǒu shíjiān de （所有 时间的）	bǎifēnzhī 百分之 sānshí 三十。
The time spent sleeping is 30% (of the total time).			
Zuò dìtiě 坐 地铁 shàngbān de rén 上班 的人	zhàn 占	suǒyǒu shàngbān （所有 上班 rénshù de 人数 的）	bǎifēnzhī 百分之 wǔshí 五十。
People who go to work by subway constitute 50% (of all the commuters).			

chúle yǐwài hái
除了……以外，还……

除了 is a preposition used before a noun, a verb or an adjective. When it is used in a sentence with **还**, **除了** means "in addition to" or "besides". The word placed after **除了** should express something that is of the same nature as what is stated in the main clause with **还**. For example,

Chúle qúnzi yǐwài tā hái mǎi le dàyī
除了 裙子 以外，她 还 买了 大衣。

Besides a skirt, she also bought an overcoat.

Chúle pǎobù yǐwài tā hái xǐhuan dǎ lánqiú
除了 跑步 以外，他 还 喜欢 打 篮球。

In addition to jogging, he also likes playing basketball.

However, if **除了** is used in a sentence without **还**, it means "except". For example,

Chúle tā suǒyǒu rén dōu qù kàn diànyǐng le
除了 他，所有 人 都 去 看 电影 了。

Everyone went to see the film except him.

Chúle Xīngqīliù yǐwài wǒ měi tiān dōu kěyǐ lái
除了 星期六（以外），我 每 天 都 可以 来。

I can come every day except Saturday.

Chúle Shuǐzhǔyú wǒ xǐhuan suǒyǒu de cài
除了 水煮鱼，我 喜欢 所有 的 菜。

I like all the dishes except the fish boiled in hot chilli oil.

Unit 10

Serial verb constructions

In serial verb constructions, the predicate of a sentence can contain more than one verb phrase describing consecutive actions. These verb phrases are related in manner or purpose, and their order cannot be changed. Usually the first verb phrase relates to manner, while the last verb phrase concerns purpose. For example,

Subject	Predicate	
	Verb phrase 1	Verb phrase 2
Zhōngguó rén 中国 人	tiē chūnlián 贴 春联 (manner)	qìngzhù xīnnián de dàolái 庆祝 新年 的到来。
Chinese people put up Spring Festival couplets to celebrate the arrival of the New Year.		
Wǒ 我	zuò huǒchē 坐 火车 (manner)	qù Běijīng 去 北京。
I took the train to Beijing.		
Wǒmen 我们	qù Wáng Yù jiā 去 王 玉 家	bàinián 拜年。(purpose)
We went to Wang Yu's home to pay a New Year visit.		
Wǒmen 我们	qù Sìchuān fànguǎn 去 四川 饭馆	chīfàn 吃饭。(purpose)
We went to a Sichuan restaurant to eat.		

Affirmative-negative questions

Affirmative-negative questions are used to ask whether something is positive or negative. The question word consists of a verb or an adjective and its negative form with **不** or **没**, for example, **好不好/看没看**. **不** is used to ask about a simple fact, while **没** is used to ask about whether something has happened or not, except when **有没有** is used to ask about possession.

Affirmative-negative questions can be used after the subject as the predicate or part of the predicate, or at the end of a statement as a follow-up question. The answer to an affirmative-negative question is either positive or negative. There is no need to provide any new information to answer such questions.

Subject	Predicate	
	Adjective/Verb	Object
Tā 他	shì bú shì 是不是	Yáo Míng 姚 明？
Is he Yao Ming?		
Nǐ 你	qù bú qù 去不去	Chéngdū 成都？
Are you going to Chengdu?		
Zhè tiáo qúnzi 这 条 裙子	hǎokàn bù hǎokàn 好看 不 好看？	
Does this skirt look nice?		
Nǐ 你	kàn méi kàn 看 没 看	diànshì 电视？
Did you watch television?		
Wáng Yù 王 玉	lái méi lái 来 没 来？	
Did Wang Yu come?		

Statement	Tag question
Zuò dìtiě qù 坐 地铁 去，	hǎo bù hǎo 好 不 好？
Going by subway—is that OK?	
Xiàwǔ sān diǎn zhōng 下午 三 点 钟，	kě bù kěyǐ 可 不 可以？
Three o'clock in the afternoon—is that possible?	
Zhè tiáo qúnzi hěn hǎokàn 这 条 裙子 很 好看，	shì bú shì 是 不 是？
This skirt is really pretty, isn't it?	

Describing immediate actions with (就)要……了 (jiù yào le)

(就)要……了 is used to indicate that an action or event is about to happen in the near future. 就 is used before 要 to emphasise the immediacy in time. Adverbs stating time are often used before (就)要 to indicate how soon the action or event is to take place. 就 is often left out in spoken Chinese and less formal situations.

Subject	Adverb	Predicate	
Wǒ 我		yào 要	huí guó le 回 国 了。
I'm going home (to my country) soon.			
Tā 她		jiù yào （就）要	xià chē le 下 车 了。
She's about to get off (the bus/train).			

Subject	Adverb	Predicate	
Wǒmen 我们	mǎshàng 马上	jiù yào （就）要	dào Chéngdū le 到 成都 了。
We're about to arrive in Chengdu.			
Shǔjià 暑假	hěn kuài 很 快	jiù yào （就）要	dào le 到 了。
The summer holidays will begin very soon.			

Unit 11

The auxiliary word 地 (de)

地 is often used after an adjective to form an adverbial phrase. It is placed before a verb to describe the manner of an action. It is part of the adverbial phrase, and cannot be placed after the verb. For example,

Subject	Modal verb	Adverbial phrase		Verb
Tā 她		hěn kuài 很 快	de 地	líkāi le 离开 了。
She left very quickly.				
Wǒmen 我们	yīnggāi 应该	jiànkāng 健康	de 地	shēnghuó 生活。
We should live healthily.				
Nǐ 你	yào 要	rènzhēn 认真	de 地	fùxí 复习。
You need to revise diligently.				

多 and 少 (duō and shǎo)

多 and 少 are two adjectives, meaning "many, much, a lot of, more" and "little, few, less" respectively. They are often used before a verb, indicating a greater or smaller quantity. For example,

Nǐ yīnggāi duō kàn, shǎo shuō
你 应该 多 看，少 说。
Keep your mouth shut and your eyes open.

Zǎofàn yào chī hǎo, wǔfàn yào chī bǎo, wǎnfàn yào chī shǎo
早饭 要 吃 好，午饭 要 吃 饱，晚饭 要 吃 少。
Have a good meal for breakfast, a heavy meal for lunch, and a light meal for supper.

Shǎo chī ròu, duō chī shūcài
少 吃 肉，多 吃 蔬菜。
Eat less meat and more vegetables.

Indicating the duration of an action

When indicating the duration of an action, the same verb is used after a verb phrase containing an object, followed by a noun phrase as the complement to denote the length of time. 了 is put after the second verb to indicate that something has already happened. For example,

Subject	Adverbial	Verb phrase	Verb	le 了	Duration
Tā 他	měi tiān 每天	kàn shū 看书	kàn 看		bàn gè 半个 xiǎoshí 小时。
He reads books for half an hour every day.					
Tā 她	xiàwǔ 下午	mǎi dōngxi 买东西	mǎi 买	le 了	liǎng gè 两个 xiǎoshí 小时。
She went shopping for two hours in the afternoon.					
Mǎkè 马克	zhōngwǔ 中午	xǐ yīfu 洗衣服	xǐ 洗	le 了	shíwǔ 十五 fēnzhōng 分钟。
Mark spent 15 minutes doing laundry at lunchtime.					
Yǒngmín 永民	zuótiān 昨天	zuò zuòyè 做作业	zuò 做	le 了	sān gè 三个 xiǎoshí 小时。
Yesterday Yeong-min did homework for three hours.					

The noun phrase denoting the length of time can also be placed between the verb and the object to act as the complement to indicate the duration of the action. If the action has already been taken, 了 must be used between the verb and the noun phrase. For example,

Subject	Adverbial	Verb	le 了	Complement	
				Noun phrase	Object
Mǎkè 马克	měi tiān 每天	kàn 看		bàn gè xiǎoshí 半个小时	de （的） shū 书。
Mark reads books for half an hour every day.					
Wáng Yù 王玉	xiàwǔ 下午	mǎi 买	le 了	liǎng gè xiǎoshí 两个小时	de （的） dōngxi 东西。
Wang Yu went shopping for two hours in the afternoon.					
Tā 他	zhōngwǔ 中午	xǐ 洗	le 了	shíwǔ fēnzhōng 十五分钟	de （的） yīfu 衣服。
He spent 15 minutes doing laundry at lunchtime.					
Tā 他	zuótiān 昨天	zuò 做	le 了	sān gè xiǎoshí 三个小时	de （的） zuòyè 作业。
Yesterday he did homework for three hours.					

Unit 12

Wh-questions

English wh-questions are called special questions in Chinese. The position of most question words in Chinese is different from the position of wh-words in English. In English, wh-words are usually placed at the beginning of questions, whereas in Chinese the question words are usually placed where the answers would be expected to appear.

Question type				
What	Zhè 这		shì 是	shénme 什么？
	What is this?			
	Zhè 这		shì 是	zhàoxiàngjī 照相机。
	This is a camera.			

Question type	
Who	Măkè shì shéi 马克 是 谁？ Who is Mark?
	Măkè shì wǒ gēge 马克 是 我 哥哥。 Mark is my elder brother.
	Shéi zhīdào zhè jiàn shì 谁 知道 这 件 事？ Who knows about this?
	Lǎoshī zhīdào zhè jiàn shì 老师 知道 这 件 事。 The teacher knows about this.
Where	Nǐ shì nǎli rén 你 是 哪里 人？ Where are you from?
	Wǒ shì Shànghǎi rén 我 是 上海 人。 I am from Shanghai.
	Nǎli yǒu mài shuǐguǒ de 哪里 有 卖 水果 的？ Where can I find a shop that sells fruit?
	Duìmiàn yǒu mài shuǐguǒ de 对面 有 卖 水果 的。 There's a place that sells fruit opposite.
When	Nǐ shénme shíhou zuò yùndòng 你 什么 时候 做 运动？ When do you do exercise?
	Wǒ měi tiān xiàwǔ zuò yùndòng 我 每 天 下午 做 运动。 I do exercise every afternoon.

Question type	
Why	Tā wèi shénme yào qǐngjià 她 为 什么 要 请假？ Why did she ask for leave?
	Tā bìng le, yào qǐngjià 她 病 了，要 请假。 She asked for leave because of illness.
How	Wǒmen zěnme qù gòuwù zhōngxīn 我们 怎么 去 购物 中心？ How do we get to the shopping centre?
	Wǒmen zuò dìtiě qù gòuwù zhōngxīn 我们 坐 地铁 去 购物 中心。 We get to the shopping centre by subway.

Difference between 有(一)点儿 (yǒuyìdiǎnr) and (一)点儿 (yìdiǎnr)

In Chinese, both 有（一）点儿 and （一）点儿 mean "a little bit". However, these phrases are used in different contexts. 有（一）点儿 can only be used before an adjective, meaning "to a small degree", and often has a negative connotation. For example, 有（一）点儿慢, 有（一）点儿急, 有（一）点儿不舒服.

When 一点儿 is used before a noun, it means the amount is not much. When 一点儿 is used after an adjective, it indicates the need for more of something.

Before a noun	
yìdiǎnr qián 一点儿钱	a little money
yìdiǎnr niúròu 一点儿牛肉	a little beef
yìdiǎnr shuǐ 一点儿水	a little water
After an adjective	
guì yìdiǎnr 贵一点儿	a bit more expensive
dà yìdiǎnr 大一点儿	a bit bigger
fāngbiàn yìdiǎnr 方便 一点儿	slightly more convenient

(一)点儿 can also be used after an adjective in a comparative structure with 比, meaning slightly higher in degree. For example,

Tā bǐ wǒ shíjì yìdiǎnr
他比我实际一点儿。

He's a little more practical than me.

Xiǎo gǒu bǐ dà gǒu kě'ài yìdiǎnr
小狗比大狗可爱一点儿。

Small dogs are a bit cuter than big dogs.

Yǒngmín bǐ Mǎkè gāo yìdiǎnr
永民 比马克 高一点儿。

Yeong-min is slightly taller than Mark.

de de de
The auxiliary words 的/地/得

Although the auxiliary words 的, 地 and 得 are all pronounced "de" with a neutral tone, they are used to form different components of a sentence.

的 is used with an adjective phrase to modify a noun. 地 is used between an adverb or adjective and a verb to describe the manner of an action. 得 is used between an adjective or verb and its complement to indicate the result or degree. For example,

Yí gè gāodà de nánrén zǒu guòlái
一个高大的男人走过来。

A big guy walked over.

Tā hěn kuài de líkāi le
他很快地离开了。

He left very quickly.

Jiànkāng de shēnghuó hěn zhòngyào
健康 地 生活 很 重要 。

Living healthily is very important.

Tā gāoxìng de xiào qǐlái
她高兴得笑起来。

She was so happy that she laughed.

Tā xiě zì xiě de hěn hǎo
他写字写得很好。

He writes very well.

Picture captions

Unit 1 p15 A stallholder paints a traditional opera mask at the Silk Market, Beijing / p18 Workers picking tea / p19 Temple of Heaven, Beijing / p20 *Baita* (White Dagoba), Beihai Park, Beijing / pp22-23 The Great Wall of China, Badaling, Beijing

Unit 2 p25 Snow-covered village in northeast China / p28 The Forbidden City, Beijing / p31 Zhujiajiao, a water village near Shanghai / pp32-33 Ice sculpture at the ice & snow festival, Harbin, Heilongjiang province

Unit 3 p35 Chinese New Year family dinner / p38 Child wearing traditional clothing with New Year lantern, Nanjing / pp42-43 Lion dance for the lantern festival in Pingliang, Gansu province

Unit 4 p45 Teenager riding a BMX bike in front of the Bell Tower, Xi'an / p48 Rickshaws in a Beijing hutong / p50 Buddhist temple on a plateau in western China / p52 Hu Jiazhi, a 112-year-old artist from Nanjing, makes a paper-cutting

Review 1 p58 Zen Buddhist temple

Unit 5 p62 The Drum Tower, Xi'an / p64 Lijiang, Yunnan province / pp66-67 Shaanxi cave dwelling

Unit 6 p69 Qin dynasty bronze chariot, Xi'an / pp70-71 Terracotta Warrior and horse, Xi'an / p72 Kneeling archer figure, Xi'an / p73 *Tangsancai* camel and musicians figurine / p75 Dragon boat race / pp76-77 Mingsha Dunes near Dunhuang, Gansu province

Unit 7 p79, 82 *Shuizhuyu*, fish in hot chilli oil, a Sichuan dish / p87 Dimsum, Cantonese food that often goes with tea

Unit 8 p89 Mosuo girl weaving cloth in her shop, Lijiang, Yunnan province / p92 Jars of green leaf tea with traditional Chinese decoration / p93 Chinese doll in traditional Qing costume / pp94-95 Qing-era bridge, Geese Springs, Guangxi Zhuang autonomous region

Review 2 p102 Victoria Harbour, Hong Kong

Unit 9 p103 Jiuzhaigou Valley, Sichuan / p104 Five-Colour Pond, Jiuzhaigou Valley / p105 Wuyi Mountain scenic area, Fujian province / pp108-109 Jiuzhaigou Valley / pp110-111 Huashan, Shaanxi province

Unit 10 p113 Woman with traditional parasol / p116 Beijing opera masks / p118 Monguor woman in traditional clothing / p119 Twin pagodas, Guilin, Guangxi Zhuang autonomous region / p120 A famous painting of Zhou Fang from the Tang dynasty / p121 Girl in Kunqu opera costume

Unit 11 p128 Statue of a crane, symbol of longevity, the Forbidden City, Beijing / pp128-129 Buddhist monks practise kung fu, Chengdu / p130 Traditional Chinese pharmacy

Unit 12 p133 Tibetan dancer / p138 Traditional doorway design / p139 Beijing opera performer in Monkey King costume / p140 Statue of Confucius at a temple in Shanghai / p142 Old man in Baoxing County, Henan province

Review 3 p145 Neighbourhood with bougainvillea and bicycles, Shenzhen, Guangdong Province / p146 Lijiang, Yunnan province

Pair work activities p149 Chinese calligraphy equipment / p151 Chinese village / p152 Chinese farmer, Yangshuo county, Guangxi Zhuang autonomous region / p153 Chinese water town / p155 Painted clay figurine / p157 Hakka fortified house, Fujian province / p158 Summer Palace, Beijing / p159 Mogao Grottoes, Dunhuang, Gansu province / p160 South Gate of the ancient city wall, Xi'an

English translations

Unit 1

Vocabulary and listening

Steve: After class, let's go and eat together. There's a Shanghai restaurant near the east gate. It's pretty good.

Amanda: I've been to that restaurant. The food there is very tasty! But I can't go today.

Steve: Why not?

Amanda: I'm going to play tennis.

Yeong-min: Really? I didn't know you could play tennis. Who are you playing with?

Amanda: With Wang Yu. She plays tennis very well. Can you play tennis?

Yeong-min: No, I can't. Steve, how about you?

Steve: I can't either. I think I should do more sport. When I lived in London, I went jogging every day before class, but I can't do that in China.

Yeong-min: Why can't you do it in China?

Steve: Because in Chinese universities classes start too early, at eight o'clock in the morning every day. I think getting out of bed to go to the classroom so early is very difficult. Of course getting up so early to go jogging is impossible!

Amanda: I think eight o'clock is not that early. I get up at seven o'clock every day, eat breakfast, then go to class.

Steve: Yeong-min, shall you and I go and eat?

Yeong-min: Sorry, my Chinese homework isn't finished, and I need to hand it in to the teacher tomorrow. I also need to do revision to prepare for the test on Wednesday.

Amanda: It doesn't matter. We can eat together next time.

Reading and writing

12th January, Wednesday

Today was really busy! I got up at half past seven, and went straight out without eating breakfast. There were lots of people on the street, and I was late. I arrived at the classroom at five past eight. The teacher had already started the lesson. I felt very embarrassed. During the lesson, the teacher had us read some stories in Chinese. Some of my classmates thought that reading stories was not useful. They like to read Chinese news. But I thought these stories were very interesting. When I have time, I want to go to the library to borrow some Chinese storybooks.

After class, I went to the park and met my friend Li Ming. The weather today was very good. We took some pretty photographs in the park. I felt very happy.

At eight o'clock in the evening, I had dinner with Wang Yu and Yeong-min. We ate and talked, and everyone was so happy. I didn't get back to the dormitory till eleven o'clock at night. I feel very tired. Once I've finished writing my diary I'll go to bed.

Unit 2

Vocabulary and listening

Amanda: Mark, why do you wear so many clothes? The weather is very nice today. The temperature is 20 degrees.

Mark: The weather here is colder than in Brisbane. So of course I have to wear a bit more.

Yeong-min: So what clothes are you going to wear when we go travelling to Xi'an? I hear the winters in Xi'an are very cold. It is very windy, and could even snow.

Amanda: I love the snow!

Mark: Snow? I could put on a few more sweaters, wear a scarf and gloves, and bring an overcoat too.

Yeong-min: How are you going to walk around if you wear so many clothes? The winter temperature in Xi'an is not too different to that in Seoul. I don't plan on bringing too many clothes.

Amanda: What's the weather like in Chengdu? Is it as cold as in Xi'an?

Yeong-min: Chengdu isn't as cold as Xi'an. Chengdu is in the south. It's warmer there than in the north.

Amanda: So I can wear my favourite T-shirt and shorts, and wear sunglasses!

Mark: I can wear surf shorts!

Yeong-min: No, no! Although Chengdu isn't as cold as Xi'an, the temperature in winter is still below ten degrees. You can't wear T-shirts and shorts. Of course, if you want to look cool, you can wear sunglasses.

Reading and writing

Weather Report

From next week onwards, cold air will affect most of the country. Due to the effects of the cold air, temperatures in the north will drop by 4~8°C. In many places the difference between daytime and nighttime temperatures will reach 10°C. The temperature difference in some places in the northwest and southwest will be over 15°C.

Xi'an

Date	Monday 7 February	Tuesday 8 February	Wednesday 9 February
Weather	Cloudy, becoming sunny	Cloudy, becoming overcast	Heavy snow
Temperature	–4°C/1°C	–5°C/2°C	–6°C/1°C

Chengdu

Date	Monday 7th February	Tuesday 8th February	Wednesday 9th February
Weather	Sunny	Cloudy, becoming overcast	Drizzle
Temperature	1°C/7°C	0°C/6°C	–2°C/6°C

Unit 3

Vocabulary and listening

Amanda: Wang Yu, happy New Year!

Wang Yu: Happy New Year! Come in, come in. Dad, Mum, my friends are here. Let me introduce you. These are my parents. These are my friends Amanda, Yeong-min and Steve.

Amanda & others: Uncle, Auntie, happy New Year!

Wang Yu's father: Happy New Year! Here are your red packets.

Amanda & others: Thanks, Uncle and Auntie.

Wang Yu's mother: Do sit down. Please have some sweets and fruit. Would you like to drink tea or fruit juice?

Amanda: I would like fruit juice.

Steve & Yeong-min: I'll have tea.

Yeong-min: Your home is very spacious and pretty.

Wang Yu: Let me show you around. This is the living room, and beside it is the dining room.

Steve: How many bedrooms are there in your home?

Wang Yu: Three. This is my elder brother's room, and opposite it is the bathroom.

Amanda: Whose room is this?

Wang Yu: That's my and my elder sister's room. My mum and dad's room is opposite.

Yeong-min: What's that delicious smell?

Wang Yu: My mum is cooking her specialty, fish in sweet-and-sour sauce. How about I take you to have a look at the kitchen?

Amanda & Steve: Great!

Reading and writing

It's New Year! by Steve

This year I spent Spring Festival in China! Spring Festival is also Chinese people's New Year, the festival when families get together. Many people put up Spring Festival couplets on the doorways of their homes, and hang red lanterns, celebrating the coming of the new year.

On the night of New Year's Eve, I went to the university's New Year's Eve party. Many of my classmates did not go home. They all stayed in Beijing for the Spring Festival. We played games and sang songs. Everyone enjoyed themselves.

On the first day of the new year, many people get up very early and go to pay New Year visits at their friends' houses. At noon, Yeong-min, Amanda and I went to Wang Yu's home for a New Year visit. First we made dumplings, then we ate. Wang Yu's mother prepared a lot of dishes. My favourite dish was the fish in sweet-and-sour sauce.

I think China's Spring Festival is both exciting and fun.

Unit 4

Vocabulary and listening

Yeong-min: Xi'an at last! After more than ten hours on a train. Oh yeah, how do we get to the Old City Hotel?

Mark: The Old City Hotel should be near the Bell Tower. Let's go outside and ask someone... Excuse me, how do we get to the Bell Tower from here? How far is it?

Passerby: The Bell Tower is in the city centre. It's quite close by, about five kilometres away. If you take a taxi you'll get there in ten minutes.

Mark: Where is the taxi rank, please?

Passerby: Go straight ahead for 50 metres, then turn right and you'll be able to see the taxi rank.

Amanda: Thank you. Do you know how to get from the city centre to the ancient city walls and the Terracotta Warriors and Horses?

Passerby: The ancient city walls are on the south side of the city centre, so you can get there on foot. The Terracotta Warriors and Horses are very far away, 30 kilometres east of Xi'an. You can go there by taxi or by bus.

Yeong-min: Does Xi'an have other interesting places?

Passerby: You ought to go to the Big Wild Goose Pagoda. It is in the south of Xi'an city.

Mark: Does the Big Wild Goose Pagoda look like a big wild goose? Haha...

Yeong-min: Mark, don't mess about.

Amanda: What about the Great Mosque?

Passerby: You should visit it too. The Great Mosque is near the Bell Tower. It's very easy to find!

Amanda: I see. Thank you so much.

Passerby: Don't mention it. I wish you a happy time in Xi'an. Goodbye.

Reading and writing

Question:

Could anyone tell me, after I arrive in Xi'an, how do I get to the Museum of Terracotta Warriors and Horses of the First Qin Emperor?

Reply:

Welcome to Xi'an!

To get to the museum, you can drive or take a taxi. You could also take the subway or go by train.

It's fast and convenient to drive or take a taxi. If there are no traffic jams, it only takes about 15 minutes to get to the motorway from the city centre. After 30 kilometres on the motorway, you come to Lintong. You exit the motorway there, and after about 10 minutes and you will arrive at the Museum of Terracotta Warriors and Horses of the First Qin Emperor. The taxi fee will be about ¥180.

It's also convenient to take the subway to get there. You will have to find the nearest subway station, transfer to Line No. 9 and get off at the Huaqingchi Station. Then take the Lintong Tourist Bus 613, which will take you to Qinyong Cun (Village of the Terracotta Warriors). Note that it could take you a long time if you have to do several subway transfers before taking the bus.

Another way is to take the train from Xi'an Station to Lintong, which takes not much more than 20 minutes. After arriving at Lintong Station, you would also take Lintong Tourist Bus 613. It's a longer journey to Qinyong Cun from Lintong Station than it is from Huaqingchi station.

Have a good time!

Unit 5

Vocabulary and listening

Receptionist: Hello! Welcome to the Old City Hotel.

Mark: Hello. We'd like to check in.

Receptionist: Do you have a reservation?

Mark: Yes, my name is Mark Johnson.

Receptionist: Could I see your passports, please?

Amanda & Yeong-min: Here you are.

Receptionist: You have reserved a standard room and a single room, for a total of four days. Is that right?

Mark: That's right.

Receptionist: Please fill in the registration card.

Mark: OK. ... Finished. There you go.

Receptionist: Thank you. ... Excuse me, is your mobile number 16628958963?

Mark: No, my mobile number is 16628958763. This is a seven, not a nine.

Receptionist: OK. Your room numbers are 826 and 832. These are the room cards.

Amanda: Excuse me, can we use the Internet in our rooms?

Receptionist: Yes, you can.

[In the room]

Receptionist: Hello! How may I help you?

Amanda: Hello! I'd like to get online, but I don't have the wifi password.

Receptionist: The password is on the back of the room card.

Amanda: Could you also give me another quilt? It's very cold here.

Receptionist: Opposite the bathroom in your room is a wardrobe. At the very top of the wardrobe there is a quilt—you can take it down and use it.

Amanda: Thank you. Goodbye.

Reading and writing

Old City Hotel

Star rating: ★★★

Area: Xi'an city centre

Address: 18 West Street, Xi'an City

Recommended — Amanda

This hotel is in the city centre. Transportation is very convenient. The rooms here are good. The bed-sheets and towels are all very clean. The basic items in the room, such as toothpaste, toothbrushes, soap, combs and so on, are all provided free. The hotel laundry service is efficient and good. I gave them an overcoat to wash in the afternoon, and by the evening it had already been cleaned. Some people think the rooms are too small, but I think the size is just right, and the room is very comfortable. Besides, I could go online in my room—it's very convenient.

Not recommended — Wang Wei

Transportation is very convenient. The service is also very good, but the rooms are too small. The room I stayed in was 3 metres long and 2.5 metres wide, much smaller than rooms in other hotels. The bed in the room is also not big enough. The single bed is 1.8 metres long and 1.2 metres wide, not big enough for a tall person.

Unit 6

Vocabulary and listening

Ticket seller: Hello.

Mark: Hello. Three student tickets, please.

Ticket seller: Could you let me see your student IDs?

Mark: Here.

Ticket seller: Thank you. Here are three tickets. It will be ¥180 in total. Your guide will wait for you at the entrance.

[Inside the museum]

Yeong-min: Excuse me, how were the Terracotta Warriors and Horses discovered?

Guide: A local farmer discovered them in 1974 while he was digging a well. This Terracotta Warrior is 1.83 metres tall, about the same height as a real person.

Amanda: Were Chinese people of that time really 1.83 metres tall? Most people aren't that tall now.

Guide: It might be a little bit taller than the people of the time.

Yeong-min: The Terracotta Warrior looks very much like our Chinese teacher—Teacher Ding. Don't you think so?

Amanda: Yes! He looks just like Teacher Ding when we haven't handed in our homework, hahaha.

Guide: Shh… Please be quieter. You can't talk loudly here.

Mark: We should take a picture for Teacher Ding.

Yeong-min: Hold on. That sign says "no photography".

Mark: Sorry, I didn't see it.

Amanda: I want to go nearer and see how tall that Terracotta Warrior is.

Mark: Don't go over there. This sign says "no entry".

Amanda: What? You're not allowed to do anything here…

Reading and writing

The Shaanxi History Museum

On our third day in Xi'an, we visited the Shaanxi History Museum. There are about 1,710,000 artefacts in the museum. It's a great place to get to know Chinese history.

There are many artefacts from the Han Dynasty (206BC–220CE) in the museum. The largest ethnic group in China, the Han, gets its name from the Han Dynasty. What the Han people speak is called *Hanyu*, and the script they use is called *Hanzi*. Of course, nowadays most Chinese people can speak *Hanyu* and write *Hanzi*.

This is an item from the Tang Dynasty (618–907CE), called *Tang San Cai*. The Tang Dynasty was one of the most prosperous eras in Chinese history. Those Chinese who went overseas long ago called themselves "Tang people". Therefore the "Chinatown" areas are also called "Tang people's streets".

Unit 7

Vocabulary and listening

[In a taxi]

Mark: Do you like Sichuan food?

Yeong-min: I like it. Sichuan food numbs your tongue and it's spicy. It's very tasty.

Amanda: You're a South Korean, so of course you like spicy food. I like Cantonese food. It's not salty or spicy. It has a comparatively light flavour.

Mark: Shanghai food is also very tasty. It's sweet and delicious.

Amanda: Don't you only love eating McDonald's and KFC?

Mark: Although I do love fast food, we ought to eat Sichuan food since we're in Sichuan.

Yeong-min: We'll arrive at the restaurant soon. ... Stop the car on the right, please.

[In the restaurant]

Waitress: How many people?

Yeong-min: Three.

Waitress: This way, please. What would you like to drink?

Mark: Please bring me a soda water.

Amanda: I would like a glass of apple juice.

Yeong-min: I'll have a glass of water.

Waitress: Here's the menu.

Yeong-min: What are your specialties?

Waitress: Mapo tofu, Kung Pao chicken, and fish boiled in hot chilli oil.

Yeong-min: We'll have those three dishes, then.

Waitress: Would you like any other dishes?

Amanda: Scrambled eggs, please—not spicy. Also, we'd like three bowls of plain rice. And please also bring us three pairs of chopsticks and three spoons.

Waitress: All right. Please wait a moment. Your food will be ready soon.

Reading and writing

Learning How to Make a Chinese Dish—Mapo Tofu

[Ingredients]

300 g tofu, 100 g minced beef (minced pork is also OK), a small amount of oil, two spoonfuls of fermented bean sauce, a small amount of seed powder of Chinese prickly ash, small amounts of spring onion, ginger and garlic, half a bowl of chicken broth

[Time]

10—15 minutes

[Cooking steps]

① Cut the tofu into small pieces. Cut the spring onion, ginger and garlic into tiny pieces.

② Put the oil into the pan, and heat it up. First add the ginger, then the meat. Stir-fry the meat until it is well done, then put it into a bowl.

③ Put oil into the pan and heat it. First put in the spring onion, ginger, garlic and fermented bean sauce and stir-fry the mixture until it gives off a fragrance. Then add the tofu and meat and stir-fry for two minutes. Add the chicken broth, and boil for five minutes. Finally, add the fine powder of Chinese prickly ash.

Unit 8

Vocabulary and listening

Stallholder: Hello! Come in and have a look.

Mark: Miss, how much is this panda?

Stallholder: Very cheap, seventy *yuan*.

Mark: That's too much. How about a bit cheaper?

Stallholder: OK, a little bit cheaper. How about fifty *yuan*?

Amanda: We're students. We don't have much money. Make it a bit cheaper still. Is thirty *yuan* OK?

Stallholder: You really can bargain. I'll sell it to you for thirty *yuan*.

Mark: Thanks. Yeong-min, do you think Wang Yu will like this panda?

Yeong-min: She'll definitely like it! But how are you going to bring it home? We already have too much luggage.

Amanda: Let's post it back. There's a post office near the hotel. I also want to send my family some postcards.

Stallholder: Is this your first time in Chengdu? You speak Putonghua very well!

Mark: Your Putonghua is very good too! What souvenir do you think our South Korean friend should buy?

Stallholder: How about this traditional Chinese jacket? The colour is very attractive, and it is very Chinese.

Yeong-min: Can I try it on?

Stallholder: No problem. This Tang jacket is real silk. It's very comfortable to wear.

Amanda: Oh, very chic! Mark, Yeong-min, I'd like to take a look over there. Let's meet back at the hotel in a while.

Mark & Yeong-min: OK, see you later!

[At the post office]

Mark: Excuse me, I'd like to send this parcel to Beijing.

Worker: You need to fill in this form. Can you read (understand) it?

Mark: No problem. … I've filled it in. Here it is.

Worker: First let's check the weight. … 1.2 kilograms. For ordinary post that's eleven *yuan*. For EMS it's twenty-seven *yuan*.

Mark: How long will ordinary post take? How long is it for EMS?

Worker: Ordinary post takes about two weeks, while EMS will get there in three days.

Mark: I'll send it by EMS. Here's the money.

Worker: Thirty *yuan*. Here's your change, three *yuan*.

Mark: Thank you. Goodbye.

Reading and writing

Wang Yu,

Hello!

Mark, Yeong-min and I have already arrived in Chengdu. Chengdu has lots of interesting scenic spots. We're all having a great time. Yesterday evening we went to eat at a restaurant near the city centre. The name of the restaurant was "Old Chengdu". We had heard that the Sichuan cuisine there was very authentic. We ordered Mapo tofu, Kung Pao chicken, and fish boiled in hot chilli oil. When we started eating I thought the flavour was very nice, but the more I ate the hotter it seemed. In the end I had to drink a big glass of water, and then I felt a bit better. But Mark and Yeong-min aren't afraid of spicy food at all. They ate up all the dishes very quickly.

This afternoon, we went shopping at a market. There are lots of things there, and they're very cheap. Yeong-min bought a Tang jacket. He looks very handsome in traditional Chinese clothes. I saw this tea set and this scarf. They're very pretty. I would like to buy one of them as a gift for your mum. Can you tell me if your mum would prefer the tea set or the scarf?

Best wishes!

Amanda

Unit 9

Vocabulary and listening

Mark: The weather's really nice today.

Yeong-min: The scenery here is amazing!

Amanda: Yes. This lake is especially pretty.

Yeong-min: Look, the water was blue just then, and now it's changed to green.

Mark: The guide book said this lake is called "Five-Colour Pond", so there ought to be five colours. I can only see two now, green and blue. The bookshop should give me a refund!

Amanda: Haha, very funny. The water over there in the lake has a lot of colours. Do you see?

Mark: I see them! Blue sky, white clouds, the multi-coloured water and green mountains. So beautiful.

Amanda: It's like a picture.

Mark: I really like this kind of natural scenery. The mountains here are particularly pretty, completely different from the mountains in Australia.

Yeong-min: They're not like the mountains in South Korea either. They're very distinctive. I've never seen scenery like this before.

Amanda: I like it here too. The air is good, and it's peaceful. Do you hear that? The birds are singing.

Mark: Haha, yes. You can't hear that in the city.

Yeong-min: Look, here are the photos that I have taken. What do you think?

Amanda: Great. Take a photo of us, please.

Yeong-min: No problem. One, two, three—smile!

Reading and writing

Wolong Reserve

The Wolong Reserve is situated to the north-west of Chengdu, approximately 130 km from Chengdu. In the reserve there are more than 100 pandas, 10% of the total number in the whole country, so it's also known as "Panda Country".

Aside from pandas, the reserve also has many other animals and plants that are protected by the state.

Transport: tourist bus (Chengdu—Wolong) 3 hours

Jiuzhaigou Valley

Jiuzhaigou is over 400 km from Chengdu. The snow-capped mountains, waterfalls, lakes and forests here are extremely beautiful. It is called "Paradise on Earth".

There are over 100 lakes, large and small, in Jiuzhaigou Valley. Among them is Five-Colour Pond, which is so clear that you can see the bottom. With the blue sky, white clouds and trees reflected in the water, it is colourful and amazing. Jiuzhaigou Valley also has many waterfalls. The widest of these waterfalls is more than 200 m wide and over 20 m high.

Transport: aeroplane (Chengdu—Jiuhuang Airport) 1 hour

tourist bus (Chengdu—Jiuzhaigou Valley) 10 hours

Unit 10

Vocabulary and listening

Amanda: I'm back! What are you two doing?

Yeong-min: We're watching TV. What souvenirs did you buy?

Amanda: I bought some silk scarves and postcards for my family. Oh, and I met two new friends.

Mark: Really?

Amanda: I'm going to meet them at a café in a while. Are you coming?

Yeong-min: I don't really feel like going. I'm very comfortable sitting here watching TV.

Amanda: My new friends are both girls.

Yeong-min: Is this café nearby?

Amanda: Ah, now you're interested! The café is behind the hotel, very close by. It only takes five minutes to walk there.

Mark: What do your new friends look like?

Amanda: One is called Lisa, and she's a German overseas student. She has long blonde hair, blue eyes and is of medium height. She's very slim. The other is called Sun Yuxiang, and she's from Shanghai. Her hair is shorter, and she's not really tall or short. She's a bit more plump than Lisa.

Mark: Sounds interesting, but you have not mentioned the most important thing.

Amanda: What's the most important thing?

Yeong-min: Mark most wants to know if they are pretty, and whether they have boyfriends!

Amanda: I'm going. If you want to know, just come with me.

Reading and writing

Amanda,

I'm very glad to know that you have arrived in Chengdu and that you're having a great time. I'd really like to see what Yeong-min looks like in traditional Chinese clothes. Very handsome, I'm sure. The two things you've chosen are both very pretty. I think my mum may like the tea set more.

Also, thanks for helping me out by taking the football kit for my cousin. Tomorrow evening he'll go to the hotel you're staying in to collect the kit. My cousin is called Wang Ming. He's 17 years old, very tall, fairly skinny, with short hair, and he wears glasses. His mobile number is 16521659870.

If you have any questions, you can call me.

Wish you a pleasant trip!

Wang Yu

Xiao Ming,

Long time no see! Are you doing well lately? Your birthday is coming. I got a friend to bring a football kit for you from Britain. It's your favourite team. The kit has two colours, blue and white, and I thought you would be a medium size. I hope you will like it.

My friend Amanda has gone on holiday to Chengdu, so I got her to bring the kit for you. Amanda is Brazilian. She isn't very tall. She has an average build, dark skin, and long hair. She's staying at Chengdu Hotel. You can go and find her at the hotel tomorrow evening. Her phone number is 16912764805.

Happy birthday!

Wang Yu

Unit 11

Vocabulary and listening

Doctor: Please sit down! What is your name?

Mark: My name is Mark.

Doctor: Whereabouts do you feel unwell?

Mark: I have a bit of a headache, a fever, and diarrhoea.

Doctor: How long has this been going on?

Mark: Two days.

Doctor: Have you been away recently?

Mark: Yes. I went travelling to Chengdu with two friends and have only just got back.

Doctor: First let's do an examination. Open your mouth wide. Let me check your throat.

Mark: Aaaaaaaah.

Doctor: Now I'll listen to your lungs.

Mark: Doctor, what disease have I caught?

Doctor: Nothing serious, just an ordinary cold. You're feeling ill because you haven't had enough rest, and you've caught a cold.

Mark: So how should it be treated? Do I need an injection?

Doctor: There's no need for an injection. I'll give you a prescription. Have a good rest, don't eat anything too spicy, and you'll be back to normal in no time.

Mark: Thank you, Doctor.

[At the dispensary]

Nurse: Mark, here's your medicine. This is medicine for your cold and to bring down the fever. Take it three times a day, two tablets each time. You can take it either before or after meals. Please note, after taking the medicine you may feel drowsy.

Mark: Thank you. Goodbye.

Reading and writing

Tips for a Healthy Life

A healthy body is very important for everyone. Do you know how to live healthily? These lifestyle tips may help you!

Is what you eat healthy?

You should eat more vegetables and fruit, and less food that has lots of oil or salt.

Do you have breakfast, lunch and dinner at fixed times and of fixed amounts?

You should have your meals at fixed times. Eat well at breakfast, eat till you're full at lunch, and eat less at dinner.

Do you drink enough water every day?

You should drink plenty of water, at least eight glasses per day.

Do you exercise often?

You should do plenty of exercise. Half an hour every day is best. Don't spend all day watching television or playing online games at home.

Do you get enough sleep every day?

Sleep early and rise early. You should sleep at least eight hours a day. Don't go to bed too late.

Unit 12

Vocabulary and listening

Amanda: Who else is coming today, Wang Yu?

Wang Yu: A good friend of mine. You can get to know each other. I think you'll like her.

Mark: Great! What's her name?

Wang Yu: Her name's Kate. She's a Canadian. She just started working in Beijing last week.

Amanda: How do you know each other?

Wang Yu: When Kate came to Beijing last year to learn Chinese, I was her teacher.

Mark: What does she look like?

Wang Yu: She has a medium figure, big blue eyes, curly and long blonde hair, and she's of the same height as me.

Amanda: She's a beautiful girl! We should introduce her to Steve and Yeong-min. By the way, what's her personality like?

Wang Yu: She's a lot like you—very optimistic, very self-confident. Although she's a little quick-tempered, she cares a lot about her friends. Kate likes making friends, and she likes singing and dancing. She can sing pop songs and folk songs. In particular, she sings the Chinese folk song "The Half-Moon Rises" very well.

Mark: Let me guess. Is she an Aries?

Wang Yu: How do you know?

Mark: I'm interested in star signs. Her personality is a lot like an Aries.

Wang Yu: You can ask her when she gets here. I hope you guessed right.

Amanda: Steve is a Leo. I heard that Leo and Aries go well together.

Wang Yu: Then we'll definitely introduce Kate and Steve to each other. Oh, do you know about the Chinese zodiac? Many people believe that the Chinese zodiac is also connected to people's personalities.

Kate: Sorry I'm late!

Reading and writing

Who am I?

1 My favourite colour is

- a red or yellow.
- b brown or grey.
- c blue or green.

2 When I go shopping, I will

- a go straight to buy what I want.
- b ask friends' opinions.
- c go to lots of different shops, comparing items and prices.

3 When I go on a summer holiday, I

- a do part-time work to earn money.
- b go travelling, mountain climbing or diving with my friends.
- c stay at home, reading books or listening to music.

4 When I'm ill, I will

- a go to see the doctor right away.
- b call my mum and ask her what to do.
- c go online to find information.

5 The pet I would most like to have is

- a a cat.
- b a dog.
- c a fish.

10–16

You are very practical and careful. You always think carefully before you act.

18–22

You like making friends very much. You care a lot about your friends, but you're not very independent.

24–30

You are very independent, self-confident and optimistic. You like an exciting life.

Pinyin pronunciation guide

Sound	Words	Example 1	Example 2
Initials			
b	bed	bō 玻	bēi 杯
p	pin	pō 坡	pāi 拍
m	moon	mō 摸	mái 埋
f	fun	fó 佛	fā 发
d	day	dé 得	dā 搭
t	tin	tè 特	tā 他
n	nose	ne 呢	nà 纳
l	long	lè 勒	lā 拉
g	good	gē 哥	gāi 该
k	kind	kē 科	kāi 开
h	hat	hē 喝	hā 哈
j	jug	jī 基	jiāo 交
q		qī 欺	qià 恰
x		xī 希	xiāo 消
zh	bridge	zhī 知	zhā 渣
ch	chin	chī 吃	chá 茶
sh	shirt	shī 诗	shā 沙
r	reduce	rì 日	rén 人
z	"ds" in reads	zī 资	zá 杂
c	"ts" in hats	cí 雌	cā 擦
s	say	sī 思	sè 色
Finals			
a	far	ā 啊	bā 八
o	saw	wō 喔	mò 墨
e	her	é 鹅	chē 车
i	bee	yī 衣	bǐ 比
u	rude	wū 乌	wū 屋
ü	German Fühlen	yū 迂	nǚ 女
ai	eye	āi 哀	bái 白
ei	eight	ēi 欸	féi 肥
ao	cow	áo 熬	bāo 包
ou	oh	ōu 欧	pōu 剖
an	enhance	ān 安	bān 班
en	taken	ēn 恩	běn 本
ang	gang	áng 昂	bāng 邦
eng	sung	hēng 亨	bēng 崩
ong	German lunge	hōng 轰	dōng 东
ia	yard	ya 呀	ph
ie	yes	yē 耶	bié 别
iao	meow	yāo 腰	jiāo 交
iu	yoga	yōu 优	diū 丢
ian	yen	yān 烟	piān 偏
in	in	yīn 因	bīn 宾
iang	e + yang	yāng 央	niáng 娘
ing	sing	yīng 英	bǐng 丙
iong	German jünger	yōng 雍	qióng 穷
ua	guano	wā 蛙	guā 瓜
uo	wall	wō 窝	duō 多
uai	why	wāi 歪	guài 怪
uei		wēi 威	wéi 围
uan	wan	wān 弯	duǎn 短
un	won	wēn 温	kūn 昆
uang	u + ongoing	wāng 汪	guāng 光
ueng		wēng 翁	wèng 瓮
üe	ü + eh	yuē 约	quē 缺
üan	ü + an	yuān 冤	xuān 宣
ün	German grün	yūn 晕	qún 群

Combinations of pinyin initials and simple finals

simple finals / Initials	a	o	e	i	u	ü
b	ba	bo		bi	bu	
p	pa	po		pi	pu	
m	ma	mo	me	mi	mu	
f	fa	fo			fu	
d	da		de	di	du	
t	ta		te	ti	tu	
n	na		ne	ni	nu	nü
l	la		le	li	lu	lü
g	ga		ge		gu	
k	ka		ke		ku	
h	ha		he		hu	
j				ji		jü (ju)
q				qi		qü (qu)
x				xi		xü (xu)

Vocabulary list

	WORD	PINYIN	PART OF SPEECH	MEANING	UNIT
A	阿姨	āyí	*n.*	aunt	3
	矮	ǎi	*adj.*	short (in stature)	10
	爱	ài	*v.*	love, like	7
	安静	ānjìng	*adj.*	quiet	6
	按时	ànshí	*adv.*	on time	11
B	巴西	Bāxī	*n.*	Brazil	10
	把	bǎ	*prep.*	(used to advance the object of a verb to the position before it)	7
	白酒	báijiǔ	*n.*	a clear Chinese liquor high in alcohol volume	7
	白天	báitiān	*n.*	daytime	2
	白羊座	báiyángzuò	*n.*	Aries	12
	百分之	bǎifēnzhī	*n.*	percent	9
	拜年	bàinián	*v.*	pay a New Year visit	3
	办理	bànlǐ	*v.*	handle	5
	帮助	bāngzhù	*v.*	help	5
	包	bāo	*v.*	wrap	3
	包裹	bāoguǒ	*n.*	parcel, package	8
	饱	bǎo	*adj.*	full, replete	11
	保护	bǎohù	*v.*	protect	9
	保护区	bǎohùqū	*n.*	conservation area	9
	杯	bēi	*n.*	cup, glass	7
	悲观	bēiguān	*adj.*	pessimistic	12
	背面	bèimiàn	*n.*	back	5
	被	bèi	*auxiliary word*	(used in the passive voice to introduce the doer of the action or the action if the doer is not mentioned)	6
	被子	bèizi	*n.*	quilt	5
	本	běn	*measure word*	(used for books)	1

* The words in colour are not target words for the units.

	WORD	PINYIN	PART OF SPEECH	MEANING	UNIT
	本地	běndì	*n.*	this locality	11
	鼻塞	bísè	*v.*	have a stuffy nose	11
	鼻子	bízi	*n.*	nose	10
	比	bǐ	*prep.*	than	2
	比较	bǐjiào	*adv.*	comparatively	4
	变成	biànchéng	*v.*	change into	9
	标准	biāozhǔn	*n./adj.*	standard	5
	表	biǎo	*n.*	form, table	8
	表弟	biǎodì	*n.*	cousin (younger male)	10
	宾馆	bīnguǎn	*n.*	hotel	4
	博物馆	bówùguǎn	*n.*	museum	4
	不错	búcuò	*adj.*	not bad	9
	不过	búguò	*conj.*	however, but	4
	不客气	bú kèqi		you're welcome	4
	不得不	bù dé bù		have no choice but to/so you have to	8
	部分	bùfen	*n.*	part	2
	不好意思	bù hǎoyìsi		(something makes you feel) embarrassed	1
	不同	bùtóng	*adj.*	different	12
C	猜	cāi	*v.*	guess	12
	才	cái	*adv.*	not until	1
	彩	cǎi	*n.*	colour	9
	菜单	càidān	*n.*	menu	7
	参加	cānjiā	*v.*	participate in, take part in	3
	餐厅	cāntīng	*n.*	dinning room	3
	差别	chābié	*n.*	difference	2
	茶	chá	*n.*	tea	3
	茶具	chájù	*n.*	tea set	8
	差不多	chàbuduō	*adj.*	about the same	2
	长	cháng	*n./adj.*	length, long	5

WORD	PINYIN	PART OF SPEECH	MEANING	UNIT
常识	chángshí	n.	general knowledge, common sense	11
朝代	cháodài	n.	dynasty	6
炒	chǎo	v.	stir-fry	7
吵架	chǎojià	v.	argue	1
车	chē	n.	carriage of a train	4
车费	chēfèi	n.	(passenger's) fare	4
称	chēng	v.	call, weigh	6
成	chéng	v.	change into	7
诚实	chéngshí	adj.	honest	12
橙子	chéngzi	n.	orange	3
池	chí	n.	pond, pool	9
迟到	chídào	v.	be late	1
宠物	chǒngwù	n.	pet	6, 12
出	chū	v.	go/come out	5
除了……以外	chúle... yǐwài		in addition, besides	9
除夕	chúxī	n.	Chinese New Year's Eve	3
穿	chuān	v.	wear (clothes)	2
床	chuáng	n.	bed	1
床单	chuángdān	n.	bedsheet	5
春节	Chūnjié	n.	Spring Festival, Chinese New Year	3
春联	chūnlián	n.	Spring Festival couplets	3
春天	chūntiān	n.	spring	2
刺激	cìjī	v.	excite	12
葱	cōng	n.	spring onion	7
聪明	cōngming	adj.	clever	12
D 达到	dádào	v.	reach	2
打工	dǎgōng	v.	do a temporary job	12
打喷嚏	dǎ pēnti		sneeze	11
打针	dǎzhēn	v.	have/give an injection	11

WORD	PINYIN	PART OF SPEECH	MEANING	UNIT
大	dà	adj.	big, large	2
大方	dàfang	adj.	generous	12
大年初一	dànián chūyī		Chinese New Year's Day	3
大约	dàyuē	adv.	approximately	4
带	dài	v.	bring, take	2
戴	dài	v.	wear (clothing accessories like hat, scarf etc)	2
单人	dānrén	n.	single person	5
当地	dāngdì	n.	local	6
当时	dāngshí	n.	that time	6
当日	dàngrì	n.	on the date stated	4
导游	dǎoyóu	n.	tour guide	6
到达	dàodá	v.	arrive	4
倒映	dàoyìng	v.	reflect, mirror	9
得病	débìng	v.	become ill	11
得名	démíng	v.	get one's name	6
德国	Déguó	n.	Germany	10
地	de	particle	(used with an adverb or adverbial phrase)	11
得	de	auxiliary word	(used between a verb or an adjective and its complement to indicate result or degree)	1
登记	dēngjì	v.	register	5
灯笼	dēnglong	n.	lantern	3
等	děng	v.	wait for	6
底	dǐ	n.	bottom	9
地道	dìdao	adj.	typical, authentic	8
地区	dìqū	n.	area	2
点	diǎn	v.	order	8
电视	diànshì	n.	TV	10
定量	dìngliàng	v./n.	fix the quantity, fixed quantity	11

WORD	PINYIN	PART OF SPEECH	MEANING	UNIT
定时	dìngshí	v./n.	fix the time, at fixed time	11
冬天	dōngtiān	n.	winter	2
懂	dǒng	v.	understand	8
豆瓣酱	dòubànjiàng	n.	fermented bean sauce	7
读	dú	v.	read	1
独立	dúlì	adj.	independent	12
堵车	dǔchē	v.	be stuck/caught in traffic	4
度	dù	n.	degree	2
肚子痛	dùzi tòng		stomach ache	11
短	duǎn	adj.	short (in length)	10
短裤	duǎnkù	n.	shorts	2
对了	duì le		by the way, that's right	10
对面	duìmiàn	n.	opposite side	3
多云	duōyún	n.	cloudy	2
E 而且	érqiě	conj.	and, but also	10
耳朵	ěrduo	n.	ear	10
二等座	èrděngzuò	n.	second-class seat	4
F 发烧	fāshāo	v.	have a fever	11
发现	fāxiàn	v.	discover	6
放	fàng	v.	put, place	7
放学	fàngxué	v.	school is over	1
非常	fēicháng	adv.	very, extremely	9
肥皂	féizào	n.	soap	5
肺	fèi	n.	lung	11
风	fēng	n.	wind	2
风景	fēngjǐng	n.	scenery	9
服务员	fúwùyuán	n.	attendant, waiter, waitress	5
服用	fúyòng	v.	take (medicine)	11
复习	fùxí	v.	revise, review	1
G 干净	gānjìng	adj.	clean	5
感觉	gǎnjué	v./n.	feel, feeling	8
感冒	gǎnmào	n./v.	cold, catch a cold	11
刚才	gāngcái	n.	just now, a moment ago	9
高速公路	gāosù gōnglù	n.	motorway, freeway	4
高铁	gāotiě		high-speed train	4
告诉	gàosu	v.	tell	8
歌曲	gēqǔ	n.	song	12
个子	gèzi	n.	height	5
更	gèng	adv.	more, even more	10
公斤	gōngjīn	measure word	kilogram	8
公里	gōnglǐ	n.	kilometre	4
狗	gǒu	n.	dog	12
够	gòu	v.	be enough	5
古	gǔ	adj.	ancient, old	4
故事	gùshi	n.	story	1
固执	gùzhi	adj.	stubborn	12
挂	guà	v.	hang up	3
拐	guǎi	v.	turn	4
关系	guānxì	n.	relationship, connection	12
关心	guānxīn	v.	caring	12
光	guāng	adj.	used up, all gone	8
光临	guānglín	v.	be present	5
锅	guō	n.	wok, pan	7
果汁	guǒzhī	n.	fruit juice	3
H 还	hái	adv.	still, yet, also	1
海浪	hǎilàng	n.	sea wave	9
海水	hǎishuǐ	n.	seawater	9
海滩	hǎitān	n.	beach	9
海外	hǎiwài	n.	overseas	6
汉语	Hànyǔ	n.	Chinese (language)	6
汉族	Hànzú	n.	Han ethnic group	6
好笑	hǎoxiào	adj.	funny	9

WORD	PINYIN	PART OF SPEECH	MEANING	UNIT
喝	hē	v.	drink	3
河流	héliú	n.	river	9
褐色	hèsè	n.	brown	10, 12
红包	hóngbāo	n.	red packet (money wrapped in red paper as a gift)	3
红茶	hóngchá	n.	black tea	7
红酒	hóngjiǔ	n.	red wine	7
喉咙	hóulóng	n.	throat	11
湖	hú	n.	lake	9
胡子	húzi	n.	moustache	10
护士	hùshi	n.	nurse	11
护照	hùzhào	n.	passport	5
花椒粉	huājiāofěn	n.	fine powder of Chinese prickly ash	7
画	huà	n.	picture	9
欢迎	huānyíng	v.	welcome	5
换乘	huànchéng		transfer	4
灰色	huīsè	n.	grey	12
J 机场	jīchǎng	n.	airport	9
鸡蛋	jīdàn	n.	(chicken's) egg	7
急	jí	adj.	irritable	12
纪念品	jìniànpǐn	n.	souvenir	8
记事本	jìshìběn	n.	notebook	8
加	jiā	v.	add	7
家	jiā	measure word	(used for families or organizations)	8
加热	jiārè	v.	heat up	7
夹克	jiākè	n.	jacket	2
间	jiān	measure word	(used for smallest units of housing)	3
检查	jiǎnchá	v.	check up, examine	11
健康	jiànkāng	adj./n.	healthy, health	11
将	jiāng	adv.	will, shall	2
姜	jiāng	n.	ginger	7
讲价	jiǎngjià	v.	bargain	8
交	jiāo	v.	hand in, submit	1
饺子	jiǎozi	n.	dumpling	3
教室	jiàoshì	n.	classroom	1
街	jiē	n.	street	5
节日	jiérì	n.	festival	3
借	jiè	v.	borrow, lend	1
介绍	jièshào	v.	introduce	3
金色	jīnsè	n.	golden, blond(e)	10
进	jìn	v.	enter, come in	3
进入	jìnrù	v.	enter	4
禁止	jìnzhǐ	v.	forbid	6
经常	jīngcháng	adv.	often	11
井	jǐng	n.	well	6
久	jiǔ	adj.	for a long time	10
就	jiù	adv.	exactly, as soon as	1
卷发	juǎnfà	n.	curly hair	12
K 咖啡	kāfēi	n.	coffee	7
开	kāi	v.	drive (a vehicle)	4
开玩笑	kāi wánxiào		make a joke	4
开心	kāixīn	adj.	happy	1
考虑	kǎolǜ	v.	consider	12
考试	kǎoshì	n.	examination, test	1
咳嗽	késou	v.	cough	11
可乐	kělè	n.	cola	7
可能	kěnéng	adj.	possible	1
克	kè	measure word	gram	7
客房部	kèfángbù	n.	guest room department	5
客厅	kètīng	n.	sitting room	3
肯德基	Kěndéjī	n.	KFC	7
空气	kōngqì	n.	air	2
哭	kū	v.	cry	1

WORD	PINYIN	PART OF SPEECH	MEANING	UNIT
块	kuài	*n.*	piece	7
快	kuài	*adj.*	fast	4
快乐	kuàilè	*adj.*	happy	1
筷子	kuàizi	*n.*	chopstick	7
宽	kuān	*n./adj.*	width, wide	5
L 拉肚子	lā dùzi		suffer from diarrhoea	11
辣	là	*adj.*	spicy, hot	7
老	lǎo	*adj.*	old	8
乐观	lèguān	*adj.*	optimistic	12
累	lèi	*adj.*	tired	1
冷	lěng	*adj.*	cold	2
梨	lí	*n.*	pear	3
离开	líkāi	*v.*	leave, exit	4
里	lǐ	*n.*	inside	5
俩	liǎ	*num.*	two (a fusion of 两 and 个)	10
连衣裙	liányīqún	*n.*	one-piece dress	2
脸	liǎn	*n.*	face	10
凉爽	liángshuǎng	*adj.*	cool	2
了解	liǎojiě	*v.*	understand	6
零下	líng xià		below zero	2
领带	lǐngdài	*n.*	tie	8
另	lìng	*pron.*	other, another	10
另外	lìngwài	*conj.*	in addition, besides	5
流鼻涕	liú bítì		have a runny nose	11
流行	liúxíng	*v.*	be popular	12
留学生	liúxuéshēng	*n.*	overseas student	10
路	lù	*n.*	bus route	4
旅游	lǚyóu	*v.*	travel	9
M 麻	má	*adj.*	(of some food) a burning sensation to the taste	7
麻烦	máfan	*v.*	bother	7

WORD	PINYIN	PART OF SPEECH	MEANING	UNIT
马上	mǎshàng	*adv.*	immediately, at once	12
卖	mài	*v.*	sell	8
麦当劳	Màidāngláo	*n.*	McDonald's	7
慢	màn	*adj.*	slow	4
忙	máng	*adj.*	busy	1
猫	māo	*n.*	cat	12
毛笔	máobǐ	*n.*	Chinese writing brush	8
毛巾	máojīn	*n.*	towel	5
毛衣	máoyī	*n.*	sweater, jumper	2
帽子	màozi	*n.*	hat	2
没错儿	méicuòr		be sure	9
没关系	méi guānxi		it doesn't matter	1
眉毛	méimao	*n.*	eyebrow	10
美	měi	*adj.*	beautiful	9
美极了	měi jí le		amazing	9
米饭	mǐfàn	*n.*	rice	7
密码	mìmǎ	*n.*	password	5
免费	miǎnfèi	*v.*	be free of charge	5
苗条	miáotiao	*adj.*	slim, slender	10
民歌	míngē	*n.*	folk song	12
民族	mínzú	*n.*	ethnic group	6
明信片	míngxìnpiàn	*n.*	postcard	8
墨镜	mòjìng	*n.*	sunglasses	2
N 拿	ná	*v.*	take, get	5
拿手菜	náshǒucài	*n.*	signature dish	3
耐心	nàixīn	*adj.*	patient	12
难	nán	*adj.*	difficult	1
能	néng	*modal v.*	can	1
鸟	niǎo	*n.*	bird	9
您	nín	*pron.*	you (respectful form)	4
牛奶	niúnǎi	*n.*	milk	7
牛肉末	niúròumò	*n.*	minced beef	7

WORD	PINYIN	PART OF SPEECH	MEANING	UNIT
牛仔裤	niúzǎikù	n.	jeans	2
农民	nóngmín	n.	farmer	6
女孩	nǚhái	n.	girl	10
暖和	nuǎnhuo	adj.	nice and warm	2
O 呕吐	ǒutù	v.	vomit	11
P 怕	pà	v.	be afraid, fear	8
旁边	pángbiān	n.	next to, beside	3
胖	pàng	adj.	plump, fat	10
配	pèi	v.	match	12
皮带	pídài	n.	leather belt	8
皮肤	pífū	n.	skin	10
脾气	píqi	n.	temper, disposition	12
皮鞋	píxié	n.	leather shoe	8
片	piàn	measure word	tablet	11
票	piào	n.	ticket	6
瓶	píng	n.	the quantity contained in a bottle, vase, jar or flask	7
苹果	píngguǒ	n.	apple	3
苹果汁	píngguǒzhī	n.	apple juice	7
平邮	píngyóu	v.	ordinary post, surface mail	8
葡萄	pútao	n.	grape	3
普通	pǔtōng	adj.	ordinary, common	11
普通话	pǔtōnghuà	n.	Putonghua	8
瀑布	pùbù	n.	waterfall	9
Q 其中	qízhōng	n.	among	8
起	qǐ	v.	begin, start	2
起床	qǐchuáng	v.	get up	1
汽水	qìshuǐ	n.	soda water	7
气温	qìwēn	n.	air temperature	2
前	qián	n.	before	1
钱包	qiánbāo	n.	wallet	8
前台	qiántái	n.	front desk	5
墙	qiáng	n.	wall	4
强盛	qiángshèng	adj.	powerful and prosperous	6
切	qiē	v.	cut	7
清澈	qīngchè	adj.	clear	9
清淡	qīngdàn	adj.	(of food) not oily or strongly flavoured	7
晴	qíng	adj.	sunny	2
庆祝	qìngzhù	v.	celebrate	3
秋天	qiūtiān	n.	autumn	2
球鞋	qiúxié	n.	gym shoe	10
球衣	qiúyī	n.	jersey, team kit for sports	10
去年	qùnián	n.	last year	12
R 让	ràng	v.	let, allow, ask	1
热	rè	adj.	hot	2
热闹	rènao	adj.	bustling	3
人间	rénjiān	n.	(human) world, the earth	9
认真	rènzhēn	adj.	serious	12
日记	rìjì	n.	diary	1
日用品	rìyòngpǐn	n.	daily necessity	5
容易	róngyì	adj.	easy	4
如果	rúguǒ	conj.	if	2
入口处	rùkǒu chù	n.	entrance	6
入住	rùzhù	v.	check in	5
S 嗓子疼	sǎngzi téng		have a sore throat	11
森林	sēnlín	n.	forest	9
沙发	shāfā	n.	sofa	5
山	shān	n.	mountain, hill	9
山水	shānshuǐ	n.	scenery with hills and water	9
商店	shāngdiàn	n.	shop	12
伤心	shāngxīn	adj.	sad	1

WORD	PINYIN	PART OF SPEECH	MEANING	UNIT
上/下车	shàng/ xià chē	v.	get on/off a vehicle	4
上床	shàngchuáng	v.	go to bed	1
上课	shàngkè	v.	attend a class	1
上网	shàngwǎng	v.	go online	5
稍	shāo	adv.	a little, slightly	7
勺子	sháozi	n.	spoon	7
少量	shǎoliàng	adj.	a small quantity of	7
身材	shēncái	n.	figure, stature	10
身体	shēntǐ	n.	body	11
声	shēng	n.	voice	6
生病	shēngbìng	v.	fall sick	11
生活	shēnghuó	n./v.	life, live	11
生气	shēngqì	adj.	angry	1
失物招领	shīwù zhāolǐng		lost and found	6
狮子座	shīzizuò	n.	Leo	12
实际	shíjì	adj.	practical	12
石头	shítou	n.	stone	9
手表	shǒubiǎo	n.	watch	8
手套	shǒutào	n.	glove	2
受	shòu	v.	suffer, be subjected to	2
瘦	shòu	adj.	thin, skinny	10
售票员	shòupiàoyuán	n.	ticket seller	6
蔬菜	shūcài	n.	vegetable	11
舒服	shūfu	adj.	comfortable	5
叔叔	shūshu	n.	uncle	3
梳子	shūzi	n.	comb	5
熟	shú	adj.	well done (cook)	7
属相	shǔxiang	n.	Chinese zodiac	12
数	shù	n.	number, figure	6
树木	shùmù	n.	tree	9
水	shuǐ	n.	water	7
水果	shuǐguǒ	n.	fruit	3

WORD	PINYIN	PART OF SPEECH	MEANING	UNIT
睡觉	shuìjiào	v.	sleep	1
说话	shuōhuà	v.	speak, talk	1
丝巾	sījīn	n.	silk scarf	10
送	sòng	v.	give (as a gift)	6
送餐服务	sòngcān fúwù	n.	room service	5
酸	suān	adj.	sour	7
蒜	suàn	n.	garlic	7
虽然	suīrán	conj.	although	2
所以	suǒyǐ	conj.	therefore	6
所有	suǒyǒu	adj.	all	8
T 太阳	tàiyáng	n.	sun	2
汤	tāng	n.	soup	7
糖	táng	n.	sugar, candy	3
糖醋鱼	tángcùyú	n.	fish in sweet-and-sour sauce	3
唐装	tángzhuāng	n.	garment in a traditional Chinese style	8
套	tào	n.	set	8
特别	tèbié	adv.	especially, particularly	9
剃须刀	tìxūdāo	n.	razor	5
天气	tiānqì	n.	weather	1
甜	tián	adj.	sweet	7
填	tián	v.	fill in	5
挑选	tiāoxuǎn	v.	choose	10
贴	tiē	v.	paste	3
听说	tīngshuō	v.	hear about	2
停	tíng	v.	stop	7
同学	tóngxué	n.	classmate	1
头发	tóufa	n.	hair	10
头痛	tóutòng	v.	have a headache	11
头晕	tóuyūn	v.	dizzy	11
图书馆	túshūguǎn	n.	library	1
团圆	tuányuán	v.	have a reunion	3

WORD	PINYIN	PART OF SPEECH	MEANING	UNIT
退钱	tuì qián		refund	9
退烧	tuìshāo	v.	bring down a fever	11
W 袜子	wàzi	n.	sock	10
外面	wàimiàn	n.	outside	4
完	wán	v.	complete	1
玩	wán	v.	play	3
玩具	wánjù	n.	toy	8
完全	wánquán	adv.	completely	9
晚	wǎn	adj.	late	11
碗	wǎn	n.	bowl	7
万	wàn	num.	ten thousand	6
围巾	wéijīn	n.	scarf	2
位	wèi	measure word	(used to refer to people)	7
味道	wèidào	n.	taste, feel (of clothes)	8
为什么	wèi shénme		why	1
卫生间	wèishēngjiān	n.	toilet	3
位于	wèiyú	v.	be located	9
文物	wénwù	n.	cultural relic	6
文字	wénzì	n.	writing, script	6
问题	wèntí	n.	question, problem	10
卧室	wòshì	n.	bedroom	3
X 西瓜	xīguā	n.	watermelon	3
吸烟	xīyān	v.	smoke (tobacco)	6
洗	xǐ	v.	wash	5
洗衣	xǐyī	v.	wash clothes	5
下次	xiàcì	n.	next time	1
下降	xiàjiàng	v.	descend, fall	2
夏天	xiàtiān	n.	summer	2
下雪	xiàxuě	v.	snow	2
先	xiān	adv.	first	3
仙境	xiānjìng	n.	paradise	9
咸	xián	adj.	salty	7
线	xiàn	n.	line	4
乡	xiāng	n.	hometown, countryside	9
香	xiāng	adj.	savoury, fragrant	3
香蕉	xiāngjiāo	n.	banana	3
相信	xiāngxìn	v.	believe	12
向	xiàng	prep.	to, towards	4
像	xiàng	v.	look like	4
小	xiǎo	adj.	small, little	2
小心	xiǎoxīn	adj.	careful	12
笑	xiào	v.	laugh, smile	1
新闻	xīnwén	n.	news	1
星座	xīngzuò	n.	constellation, star sign	12
行	xíng	v.	be all right	2
行动	xíngdòng	v./n.	act, action	12
行李	xíngli	n.	luggage	8
性格	xìnggé	n.	personality	12
兴趣	xìngqù	n.	interest	10
羞怯	xiūqiè	adj.	shy	12
休息	xiūxi	v.	rest	11
嘘	xū	interj.	shh	6
悬崖	xuányá	n.	overhanging cliff	9
Y 牙膏	yágāo	n.	toothpaste	5
牙刷	yáshuā	n.	toothbrush	5
盐	yán	n.	salt	11
研究	yánjiū	v.	research, study	12
眼睛	yǎnjing	n.	eye	10
养	yǎng	v.	raise, keep	12
样子	yàngzi	n.	appearance	8
药	yào	n.	medicine	11
夜间	yèjiān	n.	nighttime	2
衣柜	yīguì	n.	wardrobe	5
一定	yídìng	adv.	definitely, for sure	8
一共	yígòng	adv.	altogether	5

WORD	PINYIN	PART OF SPEECH	MEANING	UNIT
一会儿	yíhuìr	*n.*	a little while	8
一样	yíyàng	*adj.*	the same	2
已经	yǐjīng	*adv.*	already	1
以上	yǐshàng	*n.*	above	2
椅子	yǐzi	*n.*	chair	5
一边	yìbiān	*adv.*	while, at the same time	1
意见	yìjiàn	*n.*	opinion	12
阴	yīn	*adj.*	overcast	2
因为	yīnwèi	*conj.*	because	1
饮酒	yǐnjiǔ	*v.*	drink alcohol	6
引起睡意	yǐnqǐ shuìyì		cause drowsiness	11
饮食	yǐnshí	*n./v.*	food and drink, eat and drink	6
影响	yǐngxiǎng	*v./n.*	affect, influence	2
勇敢	yǒnggǎn	*adj.*	brave	12
用	yòng	*n./v.*	use	1
油	yóu	*n.*	oil	7
邮寄	yóujì	*v.*	send by post	8
游戏	yóuxì	*n.*	game	3
有趣	yǒuqù	*adj.*	interesting	1
有时(候)	yǒushí (hou)	*adv.*	sometimes	4
又	yòu	*adv.*	also	3
右	yòu	*n.*	the right side	4
于	yú	*prep.*	at, in	6
愉快	yúkuài	*adj.*	happy, pleasant	10
雨	yǔ	*n.*	rain	2
羽绒服	yǔróngfú	*n.*	down garment	2
雨鞋	yǔxié	*n.*	rain boot	2
雨伞	yǔsǎn	*n.*	umbrella	2
预报	yùbào	*n./v.*	forecast	2
预订	yùdìng	*v.*	reserve	5
元	yuán	*n.*	*yuan*, Chinese currency unit	4

WORD	PINYIN	PART OF SPEECH	MEANING	UNIT
原料	yuánliào	*n.*	ingredient	7
越	yuè	*adv.*	more	8
月亮	yuèliang	*n.*	moon	12
Z 再	zài	*adv.*	then, again	2
再见	zàijiàn	*v.*	goodbye	4
咱们	zánmen	*pron.*	we, us	4
早	zǎo	*adj.*	early	1
占	zhàn	*v.*	make up	9
张	zhāng	*measure word*	(used for paper, paintings etc)	6
长	zhǎng	*v.*	grow, develop	10
着凉	zháoliáng	*v.*	catch a cold	11
找	zhǎo	*v.*	look for	4
照相	zhàoxiàng	*v.*	take a photograph	9
这么	zhème	*pron.*	so, such	1
着	zhe	*auxiliary word*	(used to indicate the continuation of an action or a state)	6
真丝	zhēnsī	*n.*	real silk	8
整天	zhěngtiān	*n.*	whole day, all day	11
证	zhèng	*n.*	certificate	6
正好	zhènghǎo	*adj.*	just right	5
正在	zhèngzài	*adv.*	in the process of	3
挣钱	zhèngqián	*v.*	make money	12
之一	zhī yī	*n.*	one of	6
直接	zhíjiē	*adj.*	direct	12
植物	zhíwù	*n.*	plant	9
指示牌	zhǐshìpái	*n.*	sign, notice-board	6
治	zhì	*v.*	treat (a disease)	11
中等	zhōngděng	*adj.*	medium	10
中号	zhōnghào	*adj.*	medium size	10
种	zhǒng	*measure word*	kind, type	9
重量	zhòngliàng	*n.*	weight	8

WORD	PINYIN	PART OF SPEECH	MEANING	UNIT
重要	zhòngyào	*adj.*	important	10
猪肉	zhūròu	*n.*	pork	7
煮	zhǔ	*v.*	boil	7
祝	zhù	*v.*	wish	4
祝好	zhù hǎo		best wishes	8
注意	zhùyì	*v.*	pay attention to	11
转	zhuǎn	*v.*	turn, change	2
准备	zhǔnbèi	*v.*	prepare	1
资料	zīliào	*n.*	data, material	12
自然	zìrán	*n.*	nature	9
自信	zìxìn	*adj.*	self-confident	12

WORD	PINYIN	PART OF SPEECH	MEANING	UNIT
总机	zǒngjī	*n.*	operator	5
总是	zǒngshì	*adv.*	always	12
总数	zǒngshù	*n.*	total number	9
走路	zǒulù	*v.*	walk	4
嘴	zuǐ	*n.*	mouth	10
最后	zuìhòu	*n.*	finally	7
最近	zuìjìn	*n.*	recently	10
昨天	zuótiān	*n.*	yesterday	8
做法	zuòfǎ	*n.*	way of doing a thing	7
作业	zuòyè	*n.*	homework	1